*Writers of Wales*

Editors
MEIC STEPHENS    R. BRINLEY JONES

*Proinsias Mac Cana*

# THE
# MABINOGI

University of Wales Press

Cardiff 1992

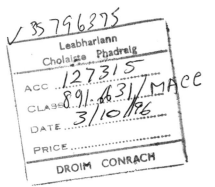

# The Mabinogi

One of the most remarkable phenomena in European history was the impact of Celtic tradition on some of the most creative literary minds of the twelfth century and after, and through them on the literature, art, and thought of European society down to our own time. The romance of Tristan and Iseult, which has its roots deep and far-spread in the traditions of Ireland and Celtic Britain, has arguably had a more profound and enduring influence on European life and art than any other secular composition. This — the *one great European myth of adultery* — was made known to the world at large through the mediation of five twelfth-century versions and promptly fired the educated imagination and established itself as a kind of archetypal paradigm of passionate love between man and woman, triggering off unending reverberations that continue to affect our assumptions about the role of love in society, whether it be in real life or expressed through the medium of art and entertainment.

Tristan's legend is associated with the much more extensive body of Arthurian romance that came to be known as the 'Matter of Britain'. The native traditions of Arthur and his ever-expanding dominium gained extraordinary acclaim and currency in the farced-up version incorporated by Geoffrey of Monmouth in his quasi-historical HISTORIA REGUM BRITANNIAE (1136–8) and fired the talents of diverse artists throughout western Europe from Chrétien de Troyes to Wagner. As re-created by Chrétien and his successors

Arthurian romance combined within it a view of courtly life and chivalry drawn largely from feudal society, a concept of courtly love blending Provençal and Celtic elements, and an imaginative, supra-natural dimension that seems to be almost wholly Celtic; and somewhere in the amalgam of these constituents lies the secret of the extraordinary attraction which these tales exerted on the collective mind of medieval Europe.

The tale of Tristan and Iseult does not fall within the scope of the present essay, for, in common with much else in early Welsh literature, it was never written — or at least has not been preserved — in an early and more or less complete form and is therefore not included in medieval manuscripts among the group of tales which have come to be known collectively as *The Mabinogi,* or *Mabinogion.* Several of these tales do, however, revolve around the adventures — and, on occasion, the misadventures — of members of the heroic company of Arthur's court. The remainder are concerned with certain specific areas of the legendary past that have — whether by historical accident or editorial design, or a combination of both — been detached from the vast web of traditional oral narrative which is postulated by innumerable references and allusions in continental Arthurian romance but which for one reason or another never acquired the permanency of the written record.

The whole cluster of tales has generally been known as *The Mabinogion* ever since Lady Charlotte Guest published her translations of them under that title during the years 1838–49, but the term is untraditional and inaccurate: the only instance of it which occurs in the manuscripts — in its Middle Welsh form *mabynnogyon* — is almost certainly a scribal error for the authentic *mabinogi*. Even this term had originally a more restricted application, referring only to the Four Branches of *Pwyll, Branwen, Manawydan* and *Math* until Lady Guest extended its scope. However, like many other misnomers of comparable status her usage is by now too well established to be summarily rejected: in the present essay my only gesture to historical accuracy will be to adopt the term *mabinogi* for her *mabinogion*. On this assumption then *The Mabinogi* comprises a medley of eleven tales: the Four Branches, just mentioned, to which the title originally referred; *Culhwch and Olwen*, a rich miscellany of romance, folklore and boisterous fantasy and the earliest extant tale to involve Arthur and his companions; *The Dream of Rhonabwy*, a retrospective and very much ironic account of an apocryphal incident during Arthur's struggle with the Saxons; the two short tales, *The Dream of Maxen Wledig* and *Lludd and Llefelys*; and the three later Arthurian romances, *Peredur Son of Efrawg, The Lady of the Fountain* (or *Owain*) and *Geraint Son of Erbin*, all of which have close counterparts in the French poetic narratives of Chrétien de Troyes.

The Welsh versions of the three romances are, be it noted, in prose, Chrétien's in verse. It is a disparity which has important implications for the history of Welsh literature and — what is of most immediate concern to us here — for the history of Welsh prose. Some schools of modern criticism would hold that a work of art should be, and should be capable of being, judged on its own terms and in isolation from contextual information but, whatever one may think of such a proposition in regard to modern, contemporary literature, few would grant it any validity in the

3

assessment of pre-modern traditional literature. For how can one, for instance, evaluate the achievement of the authors of *The Mabinogi* in comparison with other medieval prose writers unless one understands to what extent their work has been conditioned by social milieu and artistic convention; to what extent, for example, they maintain or discard the matter and the form of traditional oral literature, to what extent they reveal the influence of external models and sources, or, to return to our starting point, what are the relative roles of prose and verse in Welsh literary usage?

By its very nature prose is the more amorphous medium and its role can hardly be defined adequately except by reference to that of poetry. The latter is the eye-catching medium, above all in Wales. One is aware that Wales has its prose writers and has always had its storytellers, but one does not think of them as in any special sense typical of the community. The popular notion is that the Welsh are given to poetry and song, and, while it is arguable that their enthusiasm for choral singing is as much the product of Nonconformity as of time-old tradition, for poetry at least we have the unanimous and consistent testimony of the whole of recorded tradition in confirmation of its primacy in Welsh culture. The learned proponents of native secular tradition, however diverse or specialized their particular interests, regarded themselves primarily as poets, inspired craftsmen in words carrying with them the lingering mystique and power of their once sacred office. It is above all in poetry that the continuity of Welsh literary tradition is maintained and given visible expression, and one feels that, even in modern times, their communal interest in poetry has been for many Welshmen almost a badge of their nationhood.

The village Miltons of Wales were never mute nor would they have considered themselves inglorious — and their number was legion.

Much of the authority of poetry derives from its formal and functional definition: it is not a matter of mere chance that poetry is the characteristic medium among primitive peoples for prayer, prophecy and magic formula. Unlike a piece of prose, a poem has its shape more or less permanently fixed in terms of length, structure and metrical pattern. A medieval scribe may treat an oral prose narrative in various ways: he may expand or abbreviate, consistently or occasionally, he may paraphrase and alter the style, and so on; but with poetry his choice is generally restricted to recording it verbatim or not at all. The expert poet was a *prydydd*, 'he who imparts shape or form', and one of the terms for his art was *cerdd*, which in its broader application meant simply 'craft'. Like other crafts it had its own special terminology, and both Welsh and Irish poets had their elaborate grammars of prosody, in oral form to begin with and later in writing. Prose on the other hand, though by no means innocent of technique, was structurally free and therefore was deemed not to require, or not to merit, such technical trappings.

The greater definition of poetry declares itself again in the matter of authorship: the names of countless poets have survived throughout the centuries from the earliest age of Welsh and Irish literature, even in cases where their works have perished, whereas all the great prose works went unascribed for as long as native institutions and usage remained relatively intact. A learned poem belonged to its maker and was marked with his peculiar talent and inspiration; a prose tale, in so far as it had no fixed form and was liable to change from teller to teller, tended to be thought of as the product of an evolutionary process, so that no one version could be considered as a new creation of any individual author; instead, it was allowed to merge within the general anonymity of traditional lore.

The awareness of defined form, identity and function within an inherited and relatively unchanging social and cultural system helped to produce a profound sense of continuity in the art of poetry. As Anthony Conran has remarked:

*Tudur Aled, in the sixteenth century, shares with Taliesin, in the sixth, a common approach to verse composition that would be hard to parallel (except in Ireland) anywhere else.*[1]

This consciousness of belonging to an artistic continuum, while it may not be entirely lacking in prose, is far from being a characteristic feature of it as in the case of verse: its matter may be venerated as part of a timeless tradition, but its formulation is not.

There is, however, something of a paradox in all this. In comparison with poetry prose was amorphous and anonymous and lacked status. It could never aspire to the authority, and even sanctity, that was ascribed to poetry from the very beginning. On the other hand the Celts, the insular varieties at least, were rather exceptional among Indo-European peoples in that they used prose rather than verse for narrative purposes, and this in itself ensured to it a very important role in literature and in the transmission of received tradition; and because the Celts find themselves rather out of line in this matter one or two scholars have assumed that heroic prose narrative must be something of an innovation amongst them, replacing an older epic form.[2] But this view has little to support it except the preconception upon which it is based. The simplest and most adequate explanation would seem to be that the Celts regarded verse as the medium proper to lyric expression (allowance being made for its use as a mnemonic device in functional or canonical texts which required to be transmitted verbatim) and that for straightforward narrative they preferred prose. From the point of view of the modern reader theirs was surely the more sensible and progressive choice. Moreover, despite this functional distinction between prose and poetry — or rather because of it — the two were often combined in insular Celtic narrative: the story was told in prose, but the prose was studded with passages of verse used for heightened dialogue or to mark certain moments of tension or emotion. This union of prose and verse can be paralleled from the earliest Indian literature, and it has therefore been suggested that it is in fact the primary form of Indo-European narrative and that this has survived into medieval Welsh and Irish. The theory is attractive but not wholly convincing, particularly in view of the great frequency of *cante fable*, or narrative interspersed with song, among primitive peoples outside the Indo-European area.[3]

In any event, whether or not the theory is true, the fact is that prose narrative laced with verse passages is a well-attested form in early insular Celtic. But, such is the mutability of prose narrative that the prose may itself be drastically curtailed in writing, or even entirely omitted if chance or economy so ordains. Thus the celebrated lyric cycles of Llywarch Hen and Heledd, which Sir Ifor Williams assigned to the ninth century, survive only as long series of *englynion* or three-lined stanzas which can be divided into separate groups or poems. But as they stand they lack context, and Sir Ifor Williams has pointed out that they presuppose a linking prose narrative which has not been preserved in writing. The same pattern holds substantially true for the Welsh version of the Tristan story, which survives only in copies of the sixteenth century or later: one version, the complete one, is comprised of groups of *englynion* framed in a rather sparse prose which tells the story and which is much younger than the verse, a second merely introduces the verse with a terse and unhelpful prologue in prose, while a third is completely devoid of prose.[4] It is clear, then, that in such compositions the prose was both the staple element and the variable: without it the story as such did not exist, yet in the written text it could be reduced, recast or dropped in its entirety. In a very real sense, therefore, the primary prose narrative derived its integrity from oral tradition and the several written variants are more or less imperfect summaries of the storyteller's spoken text. In the case of the cycle of Llywarch Hen, for example, one has no good reason to suppose that the prose narrative had ever been written down, a point that has considerable importance for the history of Welsh prose.[5]

The study of early traditional literatures — of which Irish and Welsh are good examples — is beset by many difficulties. Not the least of these is the still too common misconception that literature, and most especially prose literature, only begins with writing. It is true, as any pedant can tell you, that the variants of the term found in the main European languages all derive from the Latin *litteratura* and are therefore linked from the outset with the notion of writing, but it is equally true that words outgrow their etymologies, or, as someone has expressed it in more homely terms, words mean what people want them to mean. As a minimal definition most people would accept that literature denotes conscious verbal composition of one sort or another, and on that premise those who have some acquaintance with learned or artistic oral traditions would find no *essential* difference between these and written literature apart from the accidental that one remains spoken while the other is written.

This consideration has particular significance in regard to those traditions which have been largely shaped and conserved by a class of learned men trained specifically for that purpose, as in ancient India for example, or — more apposite to our present topic — in early Ireland and Wales. Both countries had sodalities of learned poets who had once been priests and seers and who, particularly in Ireland, retained much of the trappings and prestige of their ancient office for as long as they maintained their corporate identity. It is clear from the more abundant Irish evidence that these poets cultivated and told prose narratives, not merely to entertain kings and other noble patrons, but also as an important branch of their professional learning with its varied range of myth, religion, tribal origin legends, genealogy, onomastics, and so on. At the same time there must have been a multitude of secular, unlearned storytellers of diverse talents and repertoires to cater for the interests of all sections of society. Most of the vast range of prose literature that circulated constantly among these storytellers did so only by oral transmission, even after the advent of writing, but this does not mean that it was devoid of literary style or artifice. In fact, many of the familiar features of written narrative in Irish and Welsh obviously derive from the oral prose of professional storytellers, adapted to its particular purpose and environment through age-old usage. Characteristically oral devices such as repetition, recurrent alliteration, juxtaposed synonyms, dramatic dialogue and hyperbole occur throughout Irish literature of all periods, nor are they lacking in Middle Welsh prose: clearly they had been part of the stylistic repertoire of the literary craftsman even before the advent of writing, and there is no reason to suppose that he would have been any less conscientious in their use than was the literary redactor of later centuries. For it must not be forgotten that these were conscious artists in words, learned and scrupulous — and sometimes more than a little pedantic — in their concern for language. Theirs was no primitive and untutored felicity whether in poetry or prose.

So far as Ireland is concerned, the fact is that the written prose that has been preserved in such abundance in Irish from the eighth century onwards did not spring forth from a vacuum. It represents the adaptation, more or less extensive, of a literary medium that had already behind it many centuries of evolution. *Mutatis mutandis* one would have expected a similar development in Wales.

Our earliest surviving narrative prose in Welsh is preserved in manuscripts of the Middle Welsh period and probably was not composed before approximately the beginning of the eleventh century. The exiguous prose that survives in manuscripts from before that date consists virtually of two short passages that are wholly functional and rather technical in character. Not surprisingly perhaps, the literary significance with which they have been invested is in inverse proportion to their size. The first of them, often referred to from its first word as the *Surexit* memorandum, seems to have been written before the end of the eighth century and is evidently an account of a legal case that was argued in Welsh. A number of scholars have commented on its importance as evidence for the development of Welsh prose, particularly in writing, but it could reasonably be argued that this evidence does not necessarily support the conclusions they have drawn from it. It is said, for instance, that the memorandum demonstrates that the Welsh language was already by the eighth century *an adequate medium for chronicling legal cases* and that it was even then moving from oral to written transmission, or, again, that the use of certain semi-technical phraseology shows that *a special formal language had already been developed for the purpose of legal cases.*

If one cavils at comments such as these it is not so much for what they state as for what they imply. In point of fact no one nowadays would seriously question the assumption that Welsh had developed its own special register to deal with legal matters long before the introduction of writing: internal evidence, as well as the comparative testimony of Irish and other comparable legal traditions, puts this beyond reasonable doubt. Therefore, to the extent that such a register is reflected in the memorandum, it is unnecessary to attribute this specifically to the written medium. Indeed, given the existence of a ready-made orthography — as was the case in eighth-century Wales — the problem of adapting oral to written speech is not so much that of transferring individual words and sentences from discourse to vellum as of coming to terms with a diction and style which are proper to the spoken word and adjusting the

11

prodigality of the oral mode to the unavoidable economy of the earliest manuscripts. But these difficulties are hardly faced up to in the summary transcription which is the *Surexit* memorandum; nor do they arise in the same acute form as they would if the scribe-redactor were dealing with a lengthy oral narrative with all its stylistic peculiarities and flexibilities.

The same applies to the second important piece of Old Welsh prose. This, the longest piece of continuous Old Welsh, was probably written in the tenth century and consists of twenty-three lines on the operation of the calendar. It is functional and rather mechanical in style and is evidently, if not a translation, at least a paraphrase of a written Latin source, a circumstance which renders it rather remote from the actual problem of adapting traditional narratives to the written mode. After all, direct translation of written texts is one of the most convenient ways of encouraging an entirely oral language through its first stages of literacy.

As we have seen, the oldest passage of Welsh prose is the *Surexit* memorandum, which is a summary of what was presumably an actual lawsuit. Now, given that in many early societies law is the first, or one of the first, branches of native tradition to be consigned to writing, one might perhaps infer that the memorandum is one of the first rudimentary attempts at a functional written prose in Welsh. The corollary is that a developed 'literary' or narrative prose still lay some distance in the future. Other evidence offers some support for this inference.

One formal feature of Middle Welsh prose which

differentiates it notably from that of Modern Welsh and indeed from the sparse remains of Old Welsh is the basic word-order of the sentence. Where Modern literary Welsh might have *Gwnaeth y gwas hynny* 'The groom did that' with the verb in initial position, Middle Welsh has *Y gwas a wnaeth hynny*, with the subject (or, in other instances, the object) in initial position. The important point is that this fronting of the subject or object is semantically neutral and does not confer any special emphasis on the pre-posed element; in other words, our Middle Welsh sentence means simply 'The groom did that', not 'It was the groom who did that', as Modern Welsh usage might lead us to expect. I have suggested elsewhere that the anomalous noun-initial order of Middle Welsh may be due to the influence of Late Latin on the British language, more precisely on its southern dialect.[6] Whereas the word-order noun (pronoun) + verb is the norm in Breton and Cornish, whether written or spoken, there is no evidence to suggest that it ever figured as an unmarked structure in spoken Welsh — with the significant exception of an area in south-east Glamorgan where it has been conserved in the spoken language, though in more restricted usage.[7] My suggestion is, then, that the Middle Welsh word-order in its extreme conventionalized form derives from southern British, now represented by Breton and Cornish, that it is a purely literary and written construction in Middle Welsh, and that south-east Wales provided the springboard for its extension throughout Middle Welsh prose.

The very special role which this view attributes to the south-eastern area within the Welsh context is not without precedent. Right from the beginning of history this south-eastern corner has stood somewhat apart

13

from the rest of what was later to become Wales, looking outwards rather than inwards and, by the same token, providing a gateway to external influence. Geographers have assigned it to the southern and eastern Lowland Zone of Britain as opposed to the northern and western Highland Zone to which the rest of the Welsh area belonged.[8] E.G. Bowen characterizes the cults of the saints in south-east Wales as essentially Roman or Romano-British as compared with those of the later Celtic saints in other parts of Wales.[9] He observes that this sub-area, comprising essentially the Vale of Glamorgan and Gwent, *received cultures from across the Severn Sea, or by landward penetration from Lowland Britain*, while there was continual cultural contact in prehistoric times between this area and the peninsula of south-west Britain and, via the peninsula, with Brittany.[10] Kathleen Hughes draws a similar distinction:

*The dedications of the most important saints of south-eastern Wales are concentrated in fairly confined areas: those to Dubricius mainly in Erging, those to Illtud in Glywysing, those to Cadoc mainly in Glywysing and Gwent, though with outliers. The cults of David (whose main church was St David's in the extreme south-west), Teilo (of Llandeilo Fawr in Carmarthenshire), and Beuno (of Powys stock) are, by contrast, widely scattered. This may suggest that in the Romanized areas of Wales there were strong traditions of a territorial diocese of continental type, whereas in the non-Romanized areas the monastic-type* paruchiae *carried all before them.*[11]

Nor does the special status of south-east Wales come to an end with the early historical or the prehistoric period. For example, it is now generally accepted that the three Middle Welsh romances, *Peredur Son of Efrawg*, *Owain* (or *The Lady of the Fountain*) and *Geraint*

14

*Son of Erbin*, were composed in the area comprising south-east Wales and the land around Archenfield in Herefordshire. Here there was continual intercourse between Welsh, Normans and English, not to mention the Bretons who came in the wake of William I and settled there.[12] Constance Bullock-Davies notes that Marie de France's *lais* contain details *which go a long way to prove that her original tales sprang from a local source in the Caerwent-Caerleon area.* This was part of the estate of William Consul who succeeded to the earldom of Gloucester and the lordship of Glamorgan in 1148. He was cousin to Marie, abbess of Shaftesbury, whom some scholars identify with Marie de France herself, and Dr Bullock-Davies observes that, *if Marie de France were, in truth, earl William's cousin, it would have been very easy for her to gather local stories through his household interpreter in Cardiff castle, which was his usual residence.* The association with literature was already close in the time of William's father, Robert Consul, who had been patron to William of Malmesbury, Geoffrey of Monmouth, Caradoc of Llancarfan and many other poets and writers.[13] Dr Bullock-Davies also dwells on the role of the professional interpreters in Wales during the eleventh and twelfth centuries, showing how they may have been instrumental in transmitting the *matière de Bretagne* to France, while at the same time she lays great stress on those noble households in which Normans and Welsh were united:

*Reconstruction of daily life in those great households, in which inter-marriage between French and Welsh had taken place, implies how natural the exchanging of languages and tales must have been. It points unmistakably to a way in which Celtic story could have found its way into French and then across the Border into England. Contrary to what our history textbooks sometimes infer,*

15

*because they cannot avoid over-simplification when dealing with political history on a national scale, the process of integration between Normans and Welsh and the consequent interweaving of the two cultures began much earlier than we are apt to realize. Cyfarwyddiaid, latimers, and French, Welsh and English minstrels lived together in the same castles along the Welsh Marches from the time of the Conquest. They could not have failed to impart to one another something of each of their native literatures.[14]*

One may ask what precisely is the relevance of all this to the history of Welsh prose and, more specifically, to the composition of the several narratives of *The Mabinogi*. We have seen that south-east Wales was marked off from the rest of the country by a cultural disparity which persisted from prehistoric times down to the late Middle Ages. Not merely did it receive and assimilate influences from the east; in many respects it formed part of the cultural domain of south-western Britain that comprised Cornwall and Brittany. In the eleventh and twelfth centuries it brought together Welshmen and Normans in what was evidently a fruitful union. Of the three Middle Welsh romances, one, *Owain*, is linked to the south-east by its manuscript tradition,[15] and the consensus of expert opinion tends to assign all of them to the same region. It is, therefore, rather a remarkable coincidence, to say the least, that south-eastern Welsh appears to have been aligned with Southern British in the matter of sentence word-order, which consideration in turn provides some basis for the view that this was the area from which the word-order noun (pronoun/adverb) + verb spread throughout Middle Welsh prose. That it has implications for the origins and evolution of early written narrative prose in Welsh seems very probable, but what precisely these implications are is difficult to articulate confidently at the present stage of Welsh linguistic and literary studies. The main problem is not merely that written narrative emerges into view late in the day, in the shape of *Culhwch and Olwen*, but that it emerges as it were fully formed, giving little reason to suppose that here we have the first fruits of the complex transition from oral to written storytelling. Unlike Old Irish, for which we have reasonably adequate materials by which to gauge some of the stages in the early development of written narrative, in Welsh, before *Culhwch and Olwen*, the history of written narrative is a virtual vacuum. Yet *Culhwch* can hardly have been the first of its kind. The orality of many of its components, stylistic and thematic, is palpable, but such is the author's control of the written medium, so assured and so flexible is it, that it seems to presuppose a preceding phase of trial and adaptation.

The important point here is not merely that the prose of *Culhwch and Olwen* and of medieval Welsh narrative in general is dominated by the neutral verb-second or 'abnormal' sentence but that this order seems to be specific to written Middle Welsh prose. It is not found in Old Welsh prose or in modern spoken Welsh. It is evidently not the normal sentence structure of the earliest historical poets, the *Cynfeirdd*, nor of the Court Poets of the eleventh, twelfth and thirteenth centuries, who belonged mainly to north Wales and who, in this matter as in so many others, doubtless held by the linguistic practice that they had inherited from earlier generations of poets. Thus in this one central point of Welsh syntax it would seem that Middle Welsh prose (with its later imitators) was at variance with the normal evolution of the Welsh language; in casting off the conventionalized noun-initial sentence Modern

17

Welsh prose has returned to conformity with the spoken language. Conversely the fact that it so dominates Middle Welsh prose is in itself sufficient to set it apart from the prose of our extant Old Welsh texts.

Does this mean that Middle Welsh prose narrative is in some sense an innovation, a fresh graft on the stock of Welsh literary tradition? The answer hinges very much on the status and function of prose, and especially of written prose, during the Old Welsh period, and here there is a frustrating paucity of evidence. One might perhaps draw a cautious inference from the collection of triads. Dr Bromwich has shown that the original nucleus of the TRIADS OF THE ISLAND OF BRITAIN constituted an index of oral tradition

*formed for the benefit of those whose professional duty it was to preserve and hand on the stories which embodied the oldest traditions of the Britons about themselves; stories which concerned the national past alike of the people of Wales and of the lost northern territory which was still remembered in the Middle Ages as a former home of the British race.*

In Ireland the nearest thing to this was the tale-list which existed by the tenth century and which purported to catalogue the traditional narratives that constituted the repertoire of the *fili*, or learned poet. Here the titles are arranged thematically and grouped under separate headings, such as *togla* 'destructions', *tána* 'cattle-raids', *tochmarca* 'wooings', *catha* 'battles', and so on. Clearly, therefore, in so far as the Welsh and Irish texts are intended as indexes of traditional narrative, their operating principles are wholly different: where the Irish list registers complete tales, the triads refer generally to persons, events and other component elements of tales.

Given the broad identity of purpose, the disparity between tale-list and triads is perhaps most easily explained as one of emphasis. The Irish tale-list was fitted to the needs of the learned poet *qua* storyteller and expert in tradition, whereas it seems clear from the structure and content of the triads that they were designed as a thesaurus of references for the use of the poet in his role of court poet and eulogist. The most likely inference, therefore, is that Welsh poets of the early period tended to concentrate their attention on their poetic function, especially that of praise poetry, and that in consequence they did not grant narrative prose the same status as a literary and learned genre as did their contemporaries in Ireland. All the evidence suggests that early Welsh had a rich and varied abundance of oral narrative similar to that of Irish; the fact that so much less of it has survived may be because it was not actively cultivated by the native learned class until such times as the writing of secular prose became common. This had come about in Ireland by the eighth century, and from then on there was a fruitful and continuous liaison between the monastic scriptoria and the learned poets. One of the results of this liaison was the development of variants of traditional oral prose adapted to the requirements and peculiarities of the written language.

The situation seems to have been very different in Wales. The indications are that the learned poets did not accord the same important role to prose tales in their professional repertoire as did their opposites in Ireland, while the monasteries do not appear to have interested themselves seriously in the writing of Welsh

prose narrative until the eleventh or twelfth century. For what they are worth, then, these considerations lend some further support to the view that written narrative prose is a relatively recent development in Middle Welsh.

# The Four Branches

One of the problems of the modern, non-specialized reader in approaching medieval vernacular compositions is that their idiom and background are relatively foreign and inaccessible to him. As a result he is more than normally dependent on the guidance of the expert, in this case the philologist, in forming an opinion of their artistic significance, and there is a very real danger, especially since the philologists are not automatically endowed with literary sensibility, that he will accept as canonical the views and judgements of a handful of influential scholars which have become common coinage in academic and pedagogic commentaries. The result is that he — in common indeed with many academics — tends to adopt a received, conformist appraisal of these works which precludes the flexibility of subjective reaction. It is gratifying, therefore, to see that the virtual monopoly of the Four Branches by one or two authoritative scholars is gradually being replaced in recent years by a variety of individual studies marked by mature scholarship, lack of prejudice and a keen sense of enquiry which cannot but invest the whole subject with something of the instability and changing perspective which are essential to the living appreciation of any art.

Whatever one's particular approach to medieval vernacular texts, one will normally begin by asking when they were written; only rarely in the case of prose texts can one proceed to ask by whom they were written, and it may be much more relevant to ask instead by what kind of person. In the case of the Four Branches the criteria for dating are wholly internal: the matter is drawn mainly from traditional sources, and the contemporary element betrays itself in the language and, rather less obviously, in veiled references to the contemporary situation. These constitute the evidence by which scholars have sought to assign a date to the quartet of tales.

A more or less complete text survives only in two manuscripts: the White Book of Rhydderch, dating from the last half of the fourteenth century, and the Red Book of Hergest, written sometime in the last quarter of the fourteenth century or the first quarter of the fifteenth (cf. n. 33 below), while two fragments of the second and third branches are found in Peniarth 6, a manuscript of the thirteenth century. That the composition is older than the earliest manuscript is generally agreed; by how much is still very much in question. Sir Ifor Williams adduced several linguistic features to show that the text was first written before 1100. These points are less than convincing, however, and carry less weight than his historical arguments. In the Four Branches, he maintains, stories from Gwynedd, Dyfed and Gwent have been combined in one narrative, and the most propitious time for such an undertaking during the eleventh century was between 1055 and 1062 when Gruffudd ap Llywelyn held the sovereignty of all Wales and when poets and storytellers would have been free to travel throughout the land learning the traditions and visiting the legendary sites of the other provinces. His conclusion was, therefore, that the Four Branches were probably written about 1060.

The argument is ingenious, but hardly compelling. Welsh poets and storytellers, like their Irish counterparts, were notoriously peripatetic and would have found little difficulty in receiving and transmitting literary traditions across political boundaries: one of the salient features of Celtic civilization is precisely its faculty for combining cultural unity with political disunity. But, because of the general plausibility of Sir Ifor's argument and perhaps still more because of his academic authority, there has until recently been a general consensus in favour of his suggested date. This has since been rather rudely disturbed by that brilliant author and academic nonconformist, Saunders Lewis. With characteristic panache and originality he dwells on the extent of Anglo-Norman feudal influence on the form and content of the Four Branches and relates certain incidents in the narrative to historical events of the late twelfth century.[16] On the assumption that the four tales are by the same author he would therefore date them within the period 1170–90. But his arguments have in their turn come under the searching scrutiny of T. M. Charles-Edwards, whose verdict is that they are historically either incorrect or inconclusive. His own view is that the Four Branches were written sometime between about 1050 and about 1120,[17] but he would be the first to admit that any date arrived at on the present state of the evidence can be no more than speculative, and undoubtedly Saunders Lewis's essays have done a useful service in reminding us that the date of the Four Branches is still very much an open question.

Each of the branches is rounded off by the colophon 'And thus ends this branch (cainc) of the Mabinogi', and it is from this that they have come to be known collectively as the 'Four Branches of the Mabinogi', *Pedair Cainc y Mabinogi*. Formerly it was generally accepted that the term *mabinogi* was based on the word *mab*, 'child, boy, son', and that it was used like the French *enfances* in the sense of a story about (a hero's) childhood, and the suggestion was that in this context it referred originally to the career of Pryderi son of Pwyll and Rhiannon.[18] More recently, however, Eric P. Hamp has rejected this explanation, arguing instead that the term is a collective noun based on the stem *mapono-* and that it originally meant *material or doings pertaining to (the family of) the divine Maponos (W. Mabon)*.[19] His argument is a cogent one and would seem to exclude, as he himself assumes that it does, the possibility that the cycle originally covered the career of Pryderi. On the other hand, even if the term *Mabinogi* referred initially to the traditions of the god Maponos/Mabon, by the eleventh or twelfth century it would undoubtedly have been understood as a derivative of *mab*, 'boy', and this more generalized meaning may be quite old. It is not wholly impossible, therefore, that both Eric Hamp and Ifor Williams are correct and that the title which originally denoted specifically the deeds of Maponos/Mabon came to be used subsequently in the wider sense of the deeds and career of a hero, whether Pryderi or another.[20]

In the case of the Pryderi interpretation there is of course the additional difficulty that it does not appear on the surface of the narrative, but reveals itself only after some complicated — and some might say, selective — excavation. It may be useful therefore to give an outline of the narrative before attempting to show how, in the opinion of the experts, this primary pattern has been obscured and distorted.

In the first branch Pwyll, prince of Dyfed, from whom the story takes its name, agrees to aid Arawn, king of Annwn (the Otherworld), against his rival Hafgan. He assumes his form, goes to the Otherworld, and spends the year there ruling benignly and living chastely with Arawn's wife, who seemingly never doubts his identity, though a subsequent comment makes it clear that she finds his behaviour somewhat bizarre. At the end of a year and a day he defeats Hafgan in single combat and restores the united otherworld kingdom to Arawn. Thenceforth Pwyll is called 'Head of Annwn'.

One day while sitting on the gorsedd or mound near his court at Arberth in Dyfed, Pwyll sees a beautiful maiden pass by on horseback. After several vain attempts to overtake her he prevails on her to speak with him. He learns from her that she is Rhiannon daughter of Hefeydd the Old, that she is in love with him, but that she has been promised in marriage to Gwawl son of Clud. She proposes a ruse by which Gwawl is humiliated at the wedding feast and forced to abandon his claim. Rhiannon and Pwyll are married.

After a protracted delay which causes some unease among Pwyll's subjects Rhiannon gives birth to a son. However, the baby is stolen away on the night of his birth and, in a variant of a well-known international motif, Rhiannon is accused of having murdered her own child and is subjected to a harsh and demeaning penance.

Teyrnon, lord of Gwent Is-Coed, finds an infant boy in mysterious circumstances outside his dwelling. He and his wife keep the child and name him Gwri Wallt Euryn. Eventually, however, they hear of Rhiannon's misfortune and, realizing the boy's true identity, they restore him to his parents. He is given the new name Pryderi, grows to manhood, and, on Pwyll's death, succeeds to the lordship of the seven cantrefs of Dyfed.

The second branch, Branwen Daughter of Llŷr, opens with the arrival of Matholwch, king of Ireland, at Harlech to seek Branwen daughter of Llŷr in marriage. He parleys with Bendigeidfran and Manawydan, her brothers, and the union is *arranged and duly consummated at Aberffraw in Anglesey. However, there is a fly in the ointment in the person of the irascible Efnisien, half-brother to the sons of Llŷr. He insults the Irish king by mutilating his horses and Matholwch is only prevented from departing immediately for Ireland by the promise of abundant reparation and the gift of a wondrous cauldron that had been brought from Ireland.*

*Matholwch brings Branwen to his home and eventually she gives birth to a son, who is called Gwern. Then in the following year there is a strangely delayed reaction to the insult offered to Matholwch, and Branwen is maltreated and humiliated. She sends a starling with a message to Bendigeidfran.*

*Bendigeidfran invades Ireland. When the Irish retreat across the Shannon, destroying the bridge after them, he lays himself down as a human bridge. The Irish are forced to come to terms. They plan a treacherous attack, which is thwarted by Efnisien, but battle is joined furiously when Efnisien the trouble-maker casts the child Gwern into the fire. The Irish have a cauldron of rebirth in which they revive their slain, but it is destroyed by Efnisien at the cost of his own life. The British are victorious, though only seven of them, including Manawydan son of Llŷr and Pryderi, survive the battle. Bendigeidfran, who has been wounded by a poisoned spear, asks that his head be struck off and brought to the White Mount in London.*

*When they come to Anglesey, Branwen dies of grief for the death and destruction of which she has been the unwitting cause. The seven survivors proceed on their way and, in fulfilment of Bendigeidfran's prophecy, they spend a period in Harlech and in Gwales enjoying the characteristic ease and pleasures of the Celtic Otherworld. But they violate a prohibition on opening a certain door and forthwith must abandon the paradise of Gwales and continue to London to bury the head.*

*In the third branch,* Manawydan Son of Llŷr, *Pryderi gives his mother Rhiannon in marriage to Manawydan. The whole of Dyfed becomes desolate and without habitation through a strange enchantment and Manawydan and Pryderi and their wives must seek their living for a time in England, where Manawydan distinguishes himself in turn as saddler, shield-maker and shoemaker. They return to Dyfed and, in the aftermath of a hunt, Pryderi and Rhiannon find themselves imprisoned in a magic fort which promptly vanishes in a cloud of mist.*

*Manawydan captures one of a horde of mice which consume his wheat while still on the stalk. It turns out that she is the wife of Llwyd son of Cil Coed, a friend of Gwawl son of Clud, the suitor whom Rhiannon rejected for Pwyll. Llwyd it was who cast the enchantment on Dyfed. In return for the release of his wife Manawydan compels him to lift the enchantment and release Pryderi and Rhiannon.*

*The fourth branch,* Math Son of Mathonwy, *is named after the lord of Gwynedd, whose peculiarity it is that he must keep his feet in a maiden's lap except when engaged in war. Goewin is the name of his foot-holder, and his nephew Gilfaethwy falls in love with her. Gilfaethwy's brother Gwydion devises a plan to render the maiden accessible.*

*He persuades Pryderi to exchange his marvellous swine, which had come from Annwn, for stallions and hounds which he himself had conjured up by magic and which would last but a day. The brothers return to Math's court pursued by Pryderi and Gilfaethwy sleeps with Goewin against her will.*

*The forces of Pryderi and Math join battle and Pryderi falls in single combat against Gwydion. Math punishes Gilfaethwy and Gwydion by changing them into animal form for a time.*

*Math proposes to appoint his niece Aranrhod as his new foot-holder, but when she is required to step over a wand as a test of her maidenhood, she fails dismally. She drops a yellow-haired boy-child, who goes off into the sea forthwith and is later named Dylan Eil Ton 'Son of Wave', and something else which is not then named but which turns out to be a boy who is eventually called Lleu Llawgyffes.*

*Aranrhod swears that her son will never have a name, nor bear arms, nor have a wife of mortal race, and the tale tells how Gwydion by his cunning and magic circumvents her interdiction, and in particular how he creates for Lleu a wife from the flowers of the field. But Blodeuwedd, as she is called, proves to be more beautiful than virtuous, and soon she has a lover in Gronw Pebyr and together they plot Lleu's death. Lleu is wounded but restored through Gwydion's care. Gronw is killed and Blodeuwedd turned into an owl, the enemy of all the other birds.*

The two great authorities on the study of the Four Branches were Sir Ifor Williams and W. J. Gruffydd: on the one hand the exemplary philologist who never allowed his arguments and conclusions to stray far from textual analysis, on the other the speculative enquirer who seemed sometimes to place as much store by instinct as by evidence and whose reconstructions, even at their most air-borne, have a disarming semblance of plausibility. But, despite their obvious differences of approach, there were several basic points on which they were more or less agreed: Gruffydd, for example, came to accept Williams's dating of the text, while Williams agreed with Gruffydd that in their primary form the Four Branches comprised the life cycle of the hero Pryderi, lord of Dyfed, divided into four distinct tales or branches and that in their actual form they were the work of a single redactor or author. According to Williams this author, while accepting the serial narrative of Pryderi's youth as his framework, made certain additions which in turn suggested others, producing ultimately a large composite frame-tale encompassing diverse material from Dyfed, Gwynedd and Gwent. Here again there is a substantial measure of agreement between the two scholars, though Gruffydd ventured very much further than Williams would have thought prudent or possible in seeking to chart the prehistory of the text and re-create its constituent traditions in their primitive, uncontaminated form.

Basing himself — persuasively if not always accurately — on the analogy of Irish heroic narrative, Gruffydd envisaged the primary cycle of Pryderi as comprising (*i*) the story of Pryderi's conception and birth, (*ii*) his youthful exploits, (*iii*) his rape or banishment, and finally (*iv*) his death. But the contents of these original Four Branches were progressively supplemented, and in very large measure displaced, by the intrusion of disparate themes and narrative complexes. First came the two major additions comprising the deeds of the Children of Llŷr and the Children of Dôn, both related to north Wales and mainly to Gwynedd. The Children of Llŷr, Brân (or Bendigeidfran) and Branwen, have a central role in the second branch, while the third member of the family, Manawydan, who is little more than a name in the second branch, becomes the dominant and controlling character of the third. The affairs of the family of Dôn — Gwydion, Gilfaethwy, Aranrhod and (very fleetingly) Gofannon — are confined to the fourth branch, a good part of which is also taken up with the story of the birth and career of Lleu Llawgyffes, Aranrhod's son. These more important additions were followed, evidently over a period of time, by a number of minor tales including the anecdotes of Irish origin in *Branwen* and traditional or international themes such as that of the Unfaithful Wife in the history of Lleu and Blodeuwedd in the fourth branch.

One is indeed struck even at a first reading by the range of heterogeneous materials that have gone to the making of the four tales, and it does not require a very discerning eye to see that their aggregation is secondary and that it has probably come about in several different stages. Imperfect joints in the narrative, inconsistencies and non-sequiturs, all these are sufficiently numerous to indicate diverse origins and diverse editors. Moreover there are references in earlier poetry which presuppose independent and more extended versions of episodes in the extant text, as in the boast attributed to the poet Taliesin:

*I sang before the sons of Llŷr in Ebyr Henfelen...*
[evidently a name for the Otherworld]
*I was with Brân in Ireland,*
*I saw when Morddwyd Tyllon* ['Pierced Thigh'] *was slain*

which clearly alludes to the happy Otherworld realm presided over by Brân and Manawydan and to the expedition to Ireland recounted in the second branch; or in the reflex of a variant account of the expedition, this time explicitly to the Otherworld, which is preserved in the poem *Preiddau Annwn*; or again in the reference in the same poem to the *story of Pwyll and Pryderi* which, from the indications there given, differed from that in the first branch. Much later, in the poetry of the *cywydd* period, one finds allusions to versions which do not tally with those in the extant narrative, as when Lewis Môn speaks of Aranrhod, not Goewin, as the virgin companion without whom Math could not live.

Obviously, then, a vast area of oral tradition lies behind the actual narrative and is only very inadequately reflected in it; some of its main component traditions had already, as is the wont of oral literature, generated several divergent forms and some belonged to mythological or heroic contexts quite distinct from the original framework of the Four Branches. Given the subsequent interpolation of miscellaneous matter from Irish and other sources, one can appreciate the extreme complexity of the final compilation. We shall see presently that the author of the extant text strove with very considerable skill to weld these assorted elements into a cohesive, consecutive narrative, and if he was not entirely successful this was probably due in the first place to the innate intractability of his materials and to the fact that he was attempting an ordered conflation of discrete elements such as was not — and for that matter may still not be — congenial to the Celtic artistic genius.

Matthew Arnold, whose instincts in Celtic literary matters were as sure as his knowledge of them was limited, was quick to note that the Celt lacked, or, as he put it, lacked the patience for, the sense of depth and structure, the *architectonicé*, which shapes the great works of literature, and certainly in the case of Irish literature, where the documentation is more plentiful, this is demonstrably true. The Irish had little stomach or talent for the composition *de longue haleine*: their best works are relatively short, and when they felt constrained for one reason or another to produce a composition of major dimensions, it never seems to have occurred to them that this called for new and appropriate structural modes. Instead, they tended to fill the extra space by simply multiplying the individual minor narratives and stringing them out within an essentially simple structure: in the massive Ossianic compilation of *Acallam na Senórach* 'The Converse of the Old Men' the form is that of the *Rahmenerzählung* or 'frame-story' and the linking device is topographical, the text following the peregrinations of St Patrick throughout a large part of Ireland while Oisín (or Caoilte) tells him the stories associated with its hills and rivers and plains; and in the great epic of *Táin Bó Cuailnge* 'The Cattle-raid of Cuailnge' a great deal of the actual content is accounted for by thematic repetition, particularly in the extended series of single combats between Cú Chulainn and various warriors from the army of the Connachtmen. In neither case is there any attempt at latching the several episodes together by a pattern of cross-reference or thematic reprise; Irish narrative (and *a fortiori* pre-Norman Welsh narrative) was still too close to the oral tradition to have developed a technique that smacks of the more complex mechanics of written literature.

It is very likely, then, that our author had few, if any, precedents in Welsh for the way in which he sought to splice his diverse materials into a semblance of close-knit unity. How exactly he went about his task has been pointed up very effectively in a recent study by J. K. Bollard, in which he seeks to show that the Four Branches, despite a certain apparent looseness of structure, are in reality formed to an intricate pattern which can only be *the coherent and unified work of a single artist*.[21] Bollard's argument is that the author exercised a discreet but firmly unifying control over his materials and that this is realized through a technique of interlacing such as is found in a number of other medieval compositions. What he means is best defined in his own words:

*The fact that the* Mabinogi *is grouped into four 'branches' is significant in this context, for such a grouping takes the emphasis away from the tendency to regard the tales as a linear* continuum. *The four 'branches' have the effect of presenting the tales to us much in the same way that decorative interlace designs form knots which help to create form within the interlace. The four tales are juxtaposed in order that the reader might compare the events of one with those of another, while each forms a complete tale in itself. The author expects his readers to keep in mind various themes, and when an episode arises, a slight reference to similar previous occurrences interlaces them together and we get a broader view of the entire pattern of the tales. There is no incident or detail which remains isolated or superfluous in the* Four Branches.

The process operates in two ways, one structural, the other thematic. The structural binding is achieved by the use of meaningful repetition and narrative echoes or cross-references. Thus at the beginning of the third branch Caswallawn is referred to as Manawydan's first cousin, but not actually named; for this precise identification the reader must recall a passage in the latter part of the second branch. In the third branch again, when Manawydan and Pryderi and their wives settle in Dyfed, they hold a feast and then proceed to the mound of Arberth. Both the words and the action echo the episode in *Pwyll* which prefaces the appearance of the divine Rhiannon and here also they presage the invasion of the human environment by the supernatural. As for the thematic binding, Bollard identifies the three major themes developed in the four tales as Friendships, Marriages and Feuds, and he argues very persuasively that there is a continual interplay between the three which functions as a powerful and flexible unifying element in the text as well as providing an oblique comment on social relations and attitudes. Thus Pryderi's predicament and the devastation of Dyfed in the third branch are brought about by Llwyd in revenge for the treatment of his friend Gwawl in the first and the solution comes through the good offices of the prudent Manawydan acting out of friendship for his son-in-law Pryderi, which friendship in its turn links the third branch to the second as well as to the first.

Bollard's essay is a conscious departure from the historical analysis and quest for origins which had dominated the work of Gruffydd and of most other students of the Four Branches. Where their approach is largely diachronic, his is strictly synchronic, accepting the text as it stands as a single unitary composition. Where their approach is analytic, stressing the segmental character of the text, his is synthetic, carefully assembling the elements that bespeak an overall unity. It is well justified in its results. Time and again Bollard succeeds in pointing up nuances and relations which might easily escape the casual reader or the student intent on historical analysis. For example, he reveals a subtlety in his treatment of the relationship of Pryderi and Manawydan which has not been evident in quite the same way to other observers, and we shall have reason to note further instances of his perceptiveness.

At the same time, it must be kept in mind that the Four Branches is, in one fashion or another, the product of a lengthy evolution during which it has undergone substantial changes at the hands of at least several storytellers or redactors. It still bears all the marks of a highly composite text, and it might well be argued that Bollard's preoccupation with the unifying elements produces a picture which is as incomplete, and therefore misleading, as that of the purveyors of origins. To take a specific example, he lays considerable stress in the passage already quoted on the fact that the text comprises four conjoined tales, and seems to credit this to the deliberate and sensitive craftsmanship of the author. But what exactly is the premise on which this judgement rests? Are we to take it, though he does not say so, that he rejects Gruffydd's view that the fourfold grouping reflects the four stages in Pryderi's life-cycle? Or, alternatively, that he is referring to the secondary complex of tales which now fill the original framework and that he is attributing this to the final author? If so, this is something which has not yet been demonstrated, and probably cannot be.

A further snag in the synthetic approach adopted by Bollard is that it tends to understate the breaks and inconsistencies which are quite frequent in the text. Let us take one or two examples. The story of the stealing of Rhiannon's child has been carefully analysed by Kenneth Jackson who finds that it has been constructed out of three well-known story motifs: the Calumniated Wife, the Monster Hand, and the Congenital Animals.[22] In the primary stage it told how Rhiannon's children were mysteriously stolen by a monster which was pursued by the hero (Teyrnon in the extant text) and slain. It was then disrupted by the introduction of the Congenital Animals motif, which was not integrated very happily but which explains the stealing and rescue of Teyrnon's foal and the young Pryderi's subsequent attachment to it. The final stage in what Jackson calls 'the disintegration of the tale' came with the interpolation of the motif of the Calumniated Wife charged with eating her own child. By this time the narrative was in a state of some disorder, as Jackson observes:

*It was the clumsy patching at this stage of the tale, consequent on the violent introduction of the Calumniated Wife, which has left it practically unintelligible in its present form. Who stole the child? What was this mysterious claw? Why did it steal*

*Teyrnon's foals? How did it come to drop the child in Teyrnon's stable and what was it doing there anyway? These are some of the questions which arise when we first read* Pwyll, *and the tale provides no answers — the answers are only to be found by the methods of comparative folktale study.*

By contrast Bollard brushes these difficulties aside as so many 'details' and concentrates on uncovering the positive elements in the author's handling of his text, which are very real indeed.

The danger in this is that one is prone to find what one sets out to look for. For example, Bollard comments on the 'subtle portrayal' of the relationship between Pwyll and Rhiannon when she has been accused and subjected to a humiliating penance, and then he adds:

*We learn later, when Teyrnon comes to Arberth, that not only has Pwyll chosen to keep Rhiannon with him, but that, except for the penance which she still undergoes, she has kept her position of honour in the court at Pwyll's side, for at his arrival Teyrnon is given a place of honour between them.*

Some might regard this as a pardonable inconsistency, explicable by the formulaic manner in which court seating arrangements are described in these texts or simply by the fact that the Calumniated Wife theme has been interpolated into an earlier and more conventional setting. In any event, it is doubtful whether it can reasonably be taken as evidence of the author's subtle drawing of character.

Another instance is the violent reaction of Efnisien in the second branch when he hears of Branwen's marriage to the Irish king, Matholwch. He is enraged that she should have been bestowed without his consent as kinsman and sets about mutilating Matholwch's horses. His reaction implies clearly that he knew nothing until then of Matholwch's mission, yet in the opening passage of *Branwen* he is in the company of Bendigeidfran and Manawydan when Matholwch approaches and announces his errand. The inconsistency is all the more noticeable in that the incident in question provides the *point de départ* for the whole action of the second branch.

The fact is that examples of crude joinery are numerous in the Four Branches, and if one adopts an exclusively synchronic view of style, sense and structure, then one must saddle the author with their shortcomings as well as commending him for their virtues. If, however, one takes account of the historical perspective, then most of these shortcomings — though not all — may easily be explained and perhaps excused as the product of the stage-by-stage evolution of the text. The moral is that, in dealing with a compilatory work like the Four Branches, ideally one should at one and the same time have regard to all the several different methods of assessment and interpretation. One is reminded of Wendy Doniger O'Flaherty's comment that

*in order to see the shape of a myth, one has to shine light on it from as many different sides as possible in order to illuminate its many various surfaces*

and her conviction that this is best achieved by approaching myth armed with *the toolbox of pluralism.*[23] While her prescription has particular relevance for the polyvalent character of myth, it is also, one feels, peculiarly apt for texts such as the Four Branches which in their extant form have been shaped by various discrete agents — the skills and preferences of the final author for example, the structure, style and content, and the lengthy evolution, of the traditional narrative constituents with which he worked, and, of course, the mythology which gave some of these constituents their primary meaning and motivation — so that the more comprehensive our range of perspectives on such texts, whether synchronic or diachronic, critical-aesthetic, thematic, stylistic, social-historical, oral-traditional, folkloristic or mythological, the richer and more authentic will be our reading and understanding of them. Such a holistic approach is perhaps a counsel of perfection, and it is inevitable that most commentators on the Four Branches will, for sound practical reasons, tend to adopt a single main perspective in their exploration of the text; all one can reasonably require is that each specialist recognize that his own particular approach to the text is not the only valid one, and that to proceed as if it were is to restrict needlessly our understanding of what is after all a notably heterogeneous composition.[24]

Let us take for example the second branch, which, if we accept Gruffydd's notion of its original content, has been radically transformed in its subsequent development. The suggestion is that the tale originally told of an expedition by Pryderi to the Otherworld of Annw(f)n. This would be a variant of an expedition led by Arthur which was already by about AD 900 the subject of the poem *Preiddau Annwn* and of which there is another variant in the story of *Culhwch and Olwen*. As in *Branwen*, so in *Preiddau Annwn* only seven survivors return to the Island of Britain. In the poem, as in *Culhwch*, the purpose of the adventure was to capture a wondrous cauldron belonging to the ruler of the Otherworld, though in both *Culhwch* and *Branwen*, by a conflation of supernatural and terrestrial locations which is well attested in Celtic tradition, the island of Annwfn has become the island of Ireland. In *Branwen* the expedition is led by Brân (under his emended title Bendigeidfran 'Blessed Brân'), but Pryderi is one of his companions and figures among the seven survivors. Brân's role justifies the introduction of the family of Llŷr and in particular the story of Branwen which becomes the centre-piece of the tale.

There is a suggestion of how this may have come about in an Irish analogue of the Otherworld raid. Here the heroes Cú Roí and Cú Chulainn set out to recover (or alternatively to abduct) the woman Bláithíne and to gain possession of a Cauldron of Plenty. The lady is the principal object of the quest, the cauldron a secondary but important attraction. In the original form of the Welsh tale the cauldron was the principal object, but, whether on the analogy of the Irish tale (which was almost certainly known in Wales) or of another analogue, it is possible that a redactor saw in the recovery of the lady a neat way of giving his tale variety and a more human motivation. And so Branwen displaced the cauldron — almost but not quite.

At some stage a sub-tale was introduced, almost certainly from Irish, which told of the monstrous pair Llasar Llaes Gyfnewid and his wife, whom the Irish tried to burn in an iron house but who escaped to Britain, bringing with them a cauldron of wondrous properties which they bestowed on Bendigeidfran who in turn gave it to Matholwch. This story has the kind of bizarre drama beloved of medieval audiences and readers, and it has the additional advantage of providing a neat explanation, half learned, half

39

popular, of how the Irish colonies of Wales came into being. Its inclusion meant, however, that the cauldron, which Bendigeidfran should have won by main force in Ireland, was his already long before the Irish incursion was conceived. Nevertheless, the redactor contrived that it should return to Ireland and stand at the centre of the mighty conflict, as it did in the prototype. His anxiety not wholly to jettison the old while accommodating the new is a trait he shares with many medieval redactors of traditional narrative, but in this particular instance the compromise is worked very neatly and in such a way as to provide a timely and glorious demise for the fractious Efnisien, who had by then outlived his usefulness.

The story of Branwen was transformed — not very skilfully it may be said — into a version of the Calumniated Wife theme and further padded out by material from various sources, including Irish. The aftermath of the fight in Ireland is made to encompass the double stay in the blissful Otherworld, here located in Harlech and Gwales, the two episodes probably being drawn from two different oral versions of the same Otherworld theme.[25] If one adds to all this a scatter of minor narrative elements of diverse origins, one will have a fair idea of the complexity of *Branwen* and one will appreciate Gruffydd's comment that

*the outstanding characteristic of* Branwen *is the excessively large number of 'loose ends' in the narrative and a vast amount of incoherence and confusion. In other words, the author or the cyvarwydd is dealing with material which has undergone little of the 'ironing-out' process, as compared with the equally complex material of* Math, *for instance.*[26]

40

Clearly, Gruffydd does not lay the 'incoherence' of *Branwen* fairly and squarely at the door of its author, but regards it as the product of its peculiar textual history. One can sympathize with his viewpoint, but it does bring into question the whole notion of the final redactor of the Four Branches as an 'author', a notion which Gruffydd has done more than most to popularize. If we think of the author, as most moderns do, as a writer who has complete control over his material within the limits of his talent, then assuredly the final redactor of the Four Branches is not one. If, on the other hand, we envisage him in the more strictly etymological sense of the term as one who gives increase to his subject, whether in range, in meaning, or in style, then we can concede him the title with fair confidence. It is primarily in this latter sense that Saunders Lewis, J. K. Bollard and Gruffydd himself considered him as author rather than storyteller: he endowed the matter he inherited with a certain style and a certain philosophical cast which colour all four branches and mark them out in their present form as the product of a single artistic talent.

But the matter is perhaps not quite as simple as that. In almost everything that has been written about our author's achievement, whether from a historical and textual or a synchronic and literary point of view, there is the assumption that he had some role in the compilation of the constituent materials as well as in their writing. This obviously complicates one's assessment of his work, since the greater his part in compiling the text, the greater is his responsibility for its structure as well as for its style. And yet none of the commentators — and this applies particularly to the proponents of historical analysis — has been very explicit on this point.

Gruffydd exonerates the author from serious responsibility on the grounds that

*most of the puzzling inconsequences of the Mabinogion . . . developed in the spoken cyvarwyddyd and had already entered into the totality before the author took the matter in hand. He had to make the best he could out of unpromising material which had already been distorted during the centuries when it had passed from cyvarwydd to cyvarwydd.*[27]

On the other hand he sometimes seems to credit him — if only by implication —with a more active part in assembling the various materials of his narrative:

*He based his prose epic on a series of recited tales; he makes that plain by his references to his sources,* herwydd y dyweid y cyvarwyddyd — '*as the cyvarwyddyd says', and by giving to different sections of* Branwen *their original designation.*[28]

In so far as *Branwen* is concerned, therefore, Gruffydd sees our author as being close to his sources and even in some instances as being responsible for bringing them together. In this he may well be correct for, despite the fact that many of its narrative elements are clearly traditional, one gets the impression that they have been conjoined at a much later stage than in the case of the other three branches. With the exception of *Branwen*, however, he appears in general to assume a long-drawn-out transformation of the original life-cycle of Pryderi, with the matter relating to the families of Llŷr and Dôn being introduced at a fairly early date.

By contrast, Sir Ifor Williams seems to attribute more or less the whole conflation to the final redactor, whom he describes as *editor, composer, or compiler*. And, he argues, since this is the person who *joined together the stories of Gwynedd, Dyfed and Gwent in a single narrative*, and since the bond which joins them together is the life of Pryderi, one may safely conclude that he belonged to Pryderi's homeland of Dyfed.[29] The wr ak link in this argument, particularly in the light of Gruffydd's observations, is that, with the exception of his birth, the events of Pryderi's life have been smothered under the weight of materials of northern provenance, and if the argument from local loyalty or expertise has any force, then surely an inhabitant of Dyfed would be less likely than any other to obscure the deeds of Dyfed's hero. On the other hand, there are several linguistic features in the text which might suggest that the author was a southerner.

When Professor Jackson speaks of the architects of 'the final compilation' of the Four Branches, he does so in the plural. That he should assume the participation of several compilers is not surprising, considering that his specific concern is with the international tale motifs in the text and how precisely they have been incorporated — in other words, his approach is by definition analytic and in some degree historical — but on balance it surely seems more likely that the actual text is the work of a single hand. He believes, no doubt rightly, that a good many of the interpolated narrative elements have been added by the final compilers (for which I prefer to read 'compiler'), though his analysis of *Pwyll* shows that the text has experienced at least three stages of interpolation and change.[30] But, unlike most other commentators on the Four Branches, Jackson follows the logic of his own argument: one cannot associate the author with the compilation of the text — or even with the editing of it — while absolving him from all responsibility for its shortcomings as narrative. It has become almost routine to praise him for his storytelling skill, which is rather like making virtues out of other people's vices, for, as Professor Jackson says in effect, no self-respecting oral storyteller of the present day would be content with the kind of gaps and inconsistencies which abound in the Four Branches. No, to compliment the author as storyteller is to divert attention from his real qualities as a man of literature.

He is a stylist rather than a storyteller,[31] and his style has been consciously wrought from a judicious blend of colloquial and learned techniques. It has many of the characteristic features of oral narrative. Its sentences are generally short and direct, and, as in spoken narrative, they are frequently linked by the conjunction *a(c)* 'and' or introduced by temporal adverbs:

*And he set out that night from Arberth, and came as far as Pen Llwyn Diarwya, and there he was that night. And on the morrow in the young of the day he arose and came to Glyn Cuch to loose his dogs into the wood. And he sounded his horn . . .* [32]

It makes abundant use of the affixed pronouns after verbs and prepositions, and in this it is much closer to modern spoken Welsh than is most modern Welsh prose (compare southern colloquial *'weles-i* beside learned/literary *gwelais*). It also approximates to oral storytelling in its liberal, and extremely effective, deployment of dialogue to vary and to personalize the course of the narrative. On the other hand, its normal sentence form is the rather paradoxically named 'abnormal sentence', in which the verb is regularly preceded by its subject or object and which, if my assumptions are correct, is a mark of the literary register as opposed to the colloquial register of Middle Welsh.

Yet these are but the crude ingredients of his style. What gives it its special quality is the way in which they are combined in a controlled and flexible harmony that helps disguise the structural disunities of the narrative. If there are obscurities in the sequence of events, there are none in the rhythms of his prose. Clear and economical, smooth-flowing and sinuous, despite the various features which it shares with oral narration it strikes one as the product of a sophisticated talent, more at home with Latin manuscript texts than with the oral telling of myth and saga. Most orally conditioned literature gives itself free rein in the use of repetition, hyperbole, simile and a host of other characteristic stylistic devices, culminating at moments of emotional tension or dramatic action in streams of rhetorical language richly embellished with alliterating adjectives and designed for the ear rather than for the eye. There is some of this in *Culhwch ac Olwen* and in several of the other tales of *The Mabinogi*, but in the Four Branches there is virtually none. Adjectives are used sparingly, and almost always functionally. Figurative language has hardly any place here, and one suspects that our author would have felt it unbecoming, if not slightly indecent, to indulge himself in these overtly cosmetic aspects of his art.

There is an overriding restraint and discipline in his work, an element of puritanism one might say, and he evinces little sympathy with the barbarism and rodomontade that were so much a part of medieval courtly society. In *Branwen* he reports the cruel

45

mutilation of Matholwch's horses by Efnisien, reflecting a motif which is common to all horse-riding peoples and which is attested in the Welsh laws as well as in the Life of St Cadoc by Lifris of Llancarfan, but he does not dwell on it, using it briefly and objectively as an essential element in the motivation of his narrative. He bases part of his description of Bendigeidfran crossing to Ireland on a grotesquely extravagant passage in an Irish tale,[33] but the extravagance of his account and the very notion of Bendigeidfran as a mountainous giant are at variance with the whole tone of his narrative and become strangely muted by the sobriety of his style. In following the Calumniated Wife theme in *Pwyll* he has to subject Rhiannon to the extreme penance of sitting each day by the gate and offering to carry on her back from there to the court all those who approached. It is hardly the kind of story he would have invented himself, and he betrays his slight discomfort by applying a touch of anti-deodorant before and after: he opens the passage with the statement that Rhiannon *summoned to her teachers and wise men. And as she preferred doing penance to wrangling with the women she took on her penance*, the implication being that her penance was named by those whom she had summoned and that it was therefore in a sense self-imposed;[34] and he closes it by pointing out that, even though Rhiannon offered to carry visitors on her back, *it was chance* (damwein) *that any one would permit himself to be carried* — a nice ambiguous phrase that salves the conscience without ruining the point of the story.

He has wit and understanding but not a great deal of humour.[35] His prevailing trait is a kind of *gravitas* compounded of good sense, moderation, and a feeling for the proprieties, whether of style or behaviour. It is one he shares with Manawydan, and as one reads the Four Branches one can hardly avoid the conclusion that the author has created in Manawydan a reflection of his own personality and a vehicle for his own philosophy of life. He is the pragmatist and the peacemaker. When Pryderi entered the magic court despite Manawydan's counsel and when Rhiannon taxed her husband with being disloyal to his friend because he did not hurry to his rescue, Manawydan made no protest, nor did he seek to prevent Rhiannon rushing impetuously to join Pryderi in his imprisonment. Nor did he show resentment when Cigfa, Pryderi's wife, waxed melodramatic about the danger to her virtue in being left alone with him, or when she tried, with a kind of prim suburban snobbery, to dissuade him from taking up the craft of shoemaking.

But his patience and tolerance were not born of weakness. Despite his quiet courtesy to Rhiannon and Cigfa he was not diverted from his planned course of action, and his tenacity appears at its most dogged and receives its complete vindication in the episode of the mice in the corn when he outstays and outsmarts the magic of Llwyd son of Cil Coed. Here again a familiar story motif is brought into play — the ascending series of boons of which all but the last are refused — but it is admirably adapted to the canny circumspection of Manawydan, who takes nothing for granted: not merely does he secure the release of Rhiannon and Pryderi and the raising of the enchantment from Dyfed, but he retains his bargaining counter until he extracts from Llwyd the final undertaking that there will be no revenge for this humiliation. Vengeance and feud were part of the pattern of medieval life, but Manawydan shows how they may be rejected and circumvented by the exercise of fortitude and prudence.

As J. K. Bollard has remarked, Manawydan's overriding concern in the Four Branches is with the maintenance of law and order, even if this entails acting in ways contrary to the code of a medieval nobleman. Where Pryderi and Rhiannon react to their situation with 'heroic' or instinctive action which compounds rather than resolves their problems, Manawydan chooses the role of 'Cunctator', stolid and slow-moving to the imperceptive and the impetuous, but subtle and quick-witted to those observers, in other words the readers of the Four Branches, who follow the events to their final outcome. This is precisely what D. Myrddin Lloyd has in mind when he sees in Manawydan's conduct a thoroughgoing criticism of the heroic ideal. Where the archetypal hero opts for a short life and lasting glory, Manawydan's priorities are peace and prosperity, which can only be purchased through the practice of the unheroic and somewhat prosaic virtues of prudence and tolerance. Though his origins are deep in Celtic mythology and though even in the Four Branches he retains his association with the Otherworld and gives evidence of a more than natural prescience, above all he is cast as the protagonist of reason and enlightenment in the fight against the crudities and excesses that were so much a part of the mythopoeic world of tradition.

For men of scholarship and sophistication in the eleventh or twelfth century — and especially for churchmen — this must often have been a very real and disturbing conflict. Some time in the first half of the twelfth century a new recension was made of the great Irish saga *Táin Bó Cuailnge* 'The Cattle-raid of

Cuailnge' and was written into the compendium manuscript known as the Book of Leinster. But the monastic scribe evidently had some scruples about the propriety of labouring thus to perpetuate traditions that were often barbaric and always unchristian, and he added this colophon (in Latin, significantly):

*But I who have written this story, or rather this fable, give no credence to the various incidents related in it. For some things in it are the deceptions of demons, others poetic figments; some are probable, others improbable; while still others are intended for the delectation of foolish men.*

In his case, however, he was fortified by the example of numerous generations of clerics and monastics who recorded and redacted matter that was wholly at variance with Christian belief and practice, and so his misgivings, such as they were, were easily exorcized by a pious genuflection to orthodoxy — but not before his dubious task had been well and truly finished.

The author of the Four Branches had no comparable scribal tradition to influence him, and, in any case, one feels that he was more the detached observer and manipulator of vernacular tradition than were his monastic contemporaries in Ireland. He was probably a cleric — many things in the matter and style of his composition suggest as much — and there is nothing to indicate that he had a very profound or extensive expertise in native secular tradition. For example, when in *Branwen* fighting erupts at the instigation of Efnisien, the text has this rather cryptic sentence: *And it was then that Morddwyd Tyllion said: 'Dogs of Gwern, beware of Morddwyd Tyllion' (Guern gwngwch uiwch Uordwyt Tyllyon).* The words quoted probably come from an early poem dealing with Brân's expedition similar to that cited above from the Book of Taliesin (p. 30). They yielded up their meaning to the formidable skills of Sir Ifor Williams, but in the text they are corrupt and clearly were not understood by the scribes of the White and Red Books. Whether the author of the Four Branches understood them we cannot now be sure, but evidently he had no idea who this Morddwyd Tyllion was, though we, with the benefit of hindsight and perhaps a few extra sources, can be reasonably certain that Morddwyd Tyllion was a sobriquet for Brân and that it refers to a wound in his thigh which is the antecedent of that fateful wound which incapacitated the Fisher King and several other derivatives of Brân in continental Arthurian romance.

Our author had a variety of sources at his command: apart from the traditional material on the families of Llŷr and Dôn which form the substance of his work, he draws on the legal, genealogical, triadic and proverbial tradition as well as on Irish and international story, though much of this was no doubt already embedded in the text which came to his hand; but he strikes one withal as the gifted and learned amateur, selecting and reconstructing and sewing together, yet not somehow as a participator in the integral tradition, whether because the tradition itself had become fragmented or because as a cleric and a Latin scholar (if one may presume as much) he stood outside it, however great his interest in it.

Many commentators have remarked on this residual, miscellaneous character of the Four Branches, but none in words quite so memorable as those of Matthew Arnold:

*These [Pwyll, Arawn, Teyrnon and others] are no mediaeval*

*personages; they belong to an older, pagan, mythological world. The very first thing that strikes one, in reading the 'Mabinogion', is how evidently the mediaeval story-teller is pillaging an antiquity of which he does not fully possess the secret; he is like a peasant building his hut on the site of Halicarnassus or Ephesus; he builds, but what he builds is full of materials of which he knows not the history, or knows by a glimmering tradition merely — stones 'not of this building', but of an older architecture, greater, cunninger, more majestical.*

It is true that most of the main incidents in the Four Branches belong to the mythological layer of British tradition. The family of Dôn evidently corresponds to the divine people of the Irish known as Tuatha Dé Danann, Manawydan is the British equivalent of the Irish god of the sea Manannán mac Lir, Rhiannon (from *Rīgantonā* 'Divine Queen') and Teyrnon (from *Tigernonos* 'Divine Lord') with their son Mabon (from *Maponos* 'Divine Son') are central to the whole concept of deity among the Celts, and so on. Similarly, most of the narrative revolves around familiar mythical themes of sovereignty, the Otherworld and the Birth of the Hero, and some less obvious elements may continue archaic and all but forgotten religious forms: for instance, Georges Dumézil has discussed the curious condition by which the magician-king Math is always obliged, except in time of war, to keep his feet in the lap of a virgin girl and has related it to an ancient Indo-European myth and ritual of kingship.[36] And finally, if Eric Hamp's explanation be correct, the very title *Mabinogi* derives from the mythic history of the god Mabon.

One can therefore readily understand why Brinley Rees, whose personal contribution to the study of Celtic mythology is so very considerable, should have considered it necessary to redress the balance of critical commentary in favour of the mythological reading. In a recent essay, *Ceinciau'r Mabinogi*,[37] he has demonstrated that the mythological element pervades all of the four tales and that one cannot properly evaluate them without giving it its due weight; this is precisely where the student of literature goes badly astray who pretends to judge the Four Branches by purely literary and synchronic criteria. He shows, for example, that the representation of the family of Dôn as a congeries of magicians whose activities are dyed in illusion and trickery belongs to their mythic role and that this and many other features of the narrative spring from the creativity of myth and not from that of the author.

When he goes beyond this, however, appearing to argue that the mythology of the Four Branches constitutes an articulate and intelligible whole, and particularly when he sees in it the omnipresence of the trifunctional system which Dumézil has shown to underly much of the ideology of the Indo-European peoples, then, I feel, he presses too heavily on the evidence. Be that as it may, the important consideration for us modern readers of the Four Branches is not so much the antiquity which the author pillaged for the materials of his edifice as the mind and attitude which prompted him to use them as he did. However much mythology the Four Branches contains, it is not a mythological document in any primary sense: it is a literary construct which makes use of mythological, and other, materials. Its author is not a mythographer conscientiously recording the traditions of the gods for their own sake, but a gifted writer shaping the shattered remains of a mythology to his own literary ends. Far from giving it credence, as many of his Irish contemporaries obviously do their traditions, he handles it more in the spirit of a modern dramatist selecting and adapting Greek myth as a medium already rich in associations and as a vehicle for his own comment on contemporary society.

The analogy with drama is apt in more ways than one. No one has read these tales but has been impressed by the subtle weave of dialogue that enriches the texture of the narrative and frequently blurs the distinction between the arts of the storyteller and the dramatist. It is not an invention of the author's — the more extensive Irish materials, as well as the other Middle Welsh tales, bring out clearly the Celtic storyteller's delight in the dramatic use of dialogue — but the qualities which distinguish his narrative prose — clarity, succinctness, style, and a certain intellectual subtlety — these are again present in his speech passages but enhanced by an acute sense of situation and character. There is in fact, perhaps not surprisingly, a visible correlation between the quality of his dialogue and the strength of his characterization. I have suggested elsewhere that the characters in *Branwen* lack depth and it seems to me that those who would argue otherwise have been led by the general merits of the composition to look for conscious nuances even where these do not exist; this is one of the prevailing hazards of pre-modern literary study, where reputation so often pre-empts criticism. Branwen herself seems to me a passive and colourless figure who has little of the spirit and complexity of the great heroines of Celtic literature. Efnisien dominates the tale by his actions, but even he remains a stock character with little semblance of a developed personality. When J. K. Bollard declares that he is *a complex, and in many ways, a very tragic figure* and that *the author is very concerned with the character himself* as well as with his key role in the action of the tale, this is, I fear, an instance of the modern commentator reading his own subtleties into the author's succinct and rather matter-of-fact narrative. Efnisien is indeed complex, but only in the sense that he acts with extreme inconsistency and wilfulness, in keeping with the traditional type to which he conforms. That he has the potential of tragedy is beyond question, that he achieves tragedy I find hard to accept. Even his act of final reparation, when he sacrifices himself in order to destroy the Irish Cauldron of Rebirth, is dealt with perfunctorily for what it is: a simple narrative convenience which has more to do with plot than with personality. If this is true, and if *Branwen* is indeed rather weak on character, the probable reason is that the tale itself is a collage of disparate materials marked by discontinuity and lack of internal development.

In *Manawydan* the situation is very different. Here we have a relatively simple and progressive story with few if any pointless diversions and, still more important, the author is dealing with the character whom, if I am not mistaken, he has chosen to mediate his own attitudes and philosophy of life. There is moreover a sustained and stimulating tension throughout, first in the ethical gap which sets Manawydan in firm though benign opposition to Pryderi and Rhiannon, and secondly in the more concentrated and wholly antagonistic opposition of Manawydan and Llwyd which resolves the primary opposition while vindicating Manawydan's caution. This is reflected in the dialogue, which has a purposiveness that is lacking in *Branwen*. After a brief *renvoi* to the events of the second branch the story opens with a dialogue between Pryderi and

Manawydan in which Manawydan laments his situation, bereft of his brother Bendigeidfran and subject to the will of his cousin Caswallawn, while Pryderi, assuming for the moment the author's favoured role of counsellor and reconciler, persuades him to accept the kingdom of Dyfed for his use and pleasure and to take Rhiannon in marriage. When they come from London to Dyfed there is a brief exchange in which Manawydan and Rhiannon declare their mutual affection, and finally Pryderi announces his intention of going to England to give homage to Caswallawn, an act of political accommodation which would have done justice to Manawydan himself. The whole passage has a remarkable courtliness and the three characters address one another with a restraint and mutual respect which is a far cry from the usage of traditional oral narrative. One can see why Saunders Lewis should think this the most masterly piece of creative writing in the tale and why he attributes it to the humanistic environment of the second half of the twelfth century.[38]

Apart from Manawydan, and Gwydion to some extent, the female characters are the most strongly delineated. Branwen, it is true, presents a rather negative image and Cigfa strikes one as a slight though effective vignette of a contemporary bourgeois snob, but Rhiannon, Aranrhod and Blodeuwedd are all in their different ways strong and assertive characters that lend themselves to dramatic treatment. In some ways they recall the noble women whom the poets of *amour courtois* purported to serve as their slaves or vassals, but it is more simple to take them for what they are: literary reflexes of the Celtic goddess in some of her many aspects. When Rhiannon comes from the Otherworld and chooses Pwyll for her husband, she reincarnates the goddess of sovereignty who, in taking to her a spouse, thereby ordained him legitimate king of the territory which she personified. Not only does she take the initiative in forming a marriage alliance, but she oversways her lord and her suitor and imprints her conscious dominance on all her converse with them (except for the Calumniated Wife episode, which is in any case a secondary theme). When Pwyll in his innocence allows himself to be tricked by Gwawl son of Clud into yielding her to him, she does not conceal her impatience: *'Be dull as long as you will. Never was there a man made feebler use of his wits than you have'*, and in the aftermath it is she who dictates the stratagem by which Gwawl is finally foiled. Her masterful behaviour carries over into her dealings with Manawydan in the third branch, though here the shrewd old pragmatist is more her match than the conventional heroic prince.

The fourth branch, which is the longest, the most complex, and the most dramatic, is dominated by Aranrhod and Blodeuwedd together with Gwydion. Aranrhod embodies the implacable aspects of the goddess, ruthless in the face of rebuke or rebuff, like, for example, the Irish war-god Morrígan when rejected by Cú Chulainn. One of the crucial conflicts in the tale is that between herself and Gwydion when she seeks to smother her shame by preventing her son Lleu having a name, or arms, or a wife, which would be in effect to deny him social existence. In the event, her intransigence is thwarted by the greater magic of Gwydion, who tricks her into giving Lleu a name and arms, and finally himself conjures up for him a wife from the flowers of the oak, the broom and the meadowsweet. Blodeuwedd is the Celtic goddess in her role of *femme fatale*, and more specifically as the beautiful and faithless wife who betrays her husband for a lover. Like the Irish Bláthnaid 'Little Flower' whom she resembles in name and deed she is a creature of guile and passion, but also of tragedy, for hardly has she achieved her erotic fulfilment when she is destroyed by an inexorable vengeance. It is she more than any other character who imparts to the fourth branch the dramatic colour and force which raises it above the more balanced and more unified narrative of *Manawydan*.

This formidable trio of women owes its dramatic impact more to the resonance of tradition than to the pen of the author. If Branwen is by comparison a flaccid, colourless creation, this is probably because she plays none of the independent roles that formed the traditional repertoire of the Celtic goddess; her only part was the almost wholly passive one of the Calumniated Wife, and this she performs as if she were made for misery, more in the spirit of a Cinderella than of a Deirdre or Gráinne, or indeed of a Rhiannon or Blodeuwedd.

The case of Manawydan is different; for here surely is the author's own creation — and his greatest achievement. It is hard to know how much the characterization of Manawydan leans on traditional sources, but its whole nuance seems more redolent of the eleventh or twelfth century than of mythic prehistory. Certainly it has little enough in common with the image of Manawydan's Irish counterpart, Manannán, and the evidence for the earlier conception of him in Welsh is lamentably sparse. In a poem in the Black Book of Carmarthen he is credited with being 'profound of counsel' (*oet duis y cusil*), but to ascribe great wisdom and knowledge to Celtic as to other deities is commonplace and one should not attach too much special significance to this particular instance. It is not, however, inconceivable that the author's development of Manawydan's character, and indeed his choice of Manawydan as the exponent of his own philosophy, was inspired in the first place by this reference in a poem with which he was undoubtedly acquainted. However that may be, the Manawydan of the third branch seems to me to exemplify all the author's principal virtues, and also perhaps his limitations. One pictures the author as a cleric, learned in Latin and reasonably well informed, if not professionally expert in vernacular literature, an apostle (if that is not too dramatic a word) of tolerance and moderation for whom morality and good sense were close neighbours, sagacious and quick-witted and endowed above all with a superb sense of style. In his narrative and use of character, particularly in the case of Manawydan, he subtly conveys a scale of values which, by implication, he commends to the practice of contemporary society. For the exaggerated and impulsive ideals of heroic tradition — and, one suspects, of much of contemporary life — he projects the more Christian and more practical virtues of patience and compromise. These values are mirrored in the clear, restrained perfection of his prose.

In the final issue, literary assessments must be subjective, and for me the great accomplishment of the author of the Four Branches lies, not in his ability to structure a convincing narrative from diverse materials, for in this he is far from faultless, but in his complete and easy control of the quieter rhythms of Welsh prose and in his capacity to communicate through traditional materials not primarily of his own making a personal view of life that had relevance to the social and political situation of his time. For some readers, however, his very consistency constitutes the measure and the limit of his achievement. They miss the waywardness, the spates of hyperbole, the spontaneous flashes of lyricism, that are so much a part of the integral Celtic tradition. Had our author written all the tales of *The Mabinogi*, we would, I fear, find his very virtues becoming a little leaden through excessive familiarity. Fortunately there were other and diverse talents at work creating the varied prose literature that provides a setting for his *chef-d'oeuvre*.

# Culhwch and Olwen

It could be argued that the Four Branches is not particularly representative of the Celtic genius: its primary qualities are such as are not popularly regarded as typically Celtic, while it is largely innocent of some of those which are. Colour, lyricism, rhetoric, ebullience, these and many other traits considered characteristic of the Celtic imagination from the time of Posidonius to the present day, while they are perhaps not entirely lacking in the Four Branches, are certainly not among its salient features. They are more notably present, however, in some of the other tales of *The Mabinogi*, and it is useful to review these texts occasionally as a counterweight to any undue concentration on the Four Branches and to remind ourselves of the considerable range and variety of Middle Welsh narrative.

*Culhwch and Olwen* may have been written in the eleventh century; in any case it is probably the earliest of the Middle Welsh prose tales.[39] In many ways it is the antithesis of the Four Branches: whereas the latter cloaks its many obscurities and inconsistencies with an air of discipline and order, the former has an outward appearance of fluidity and spontaneity which conceals a precise inner structure. The central plot conforms to a well-known international folktale in which the hero sets out to find and marry the daughter of a king or giant who imposes a series of difficult tasks upon her suitors and puts them to death when, inevitably, they fail to accomplish them. With the aid of helping companions possessed of magic skills the actual hero succeeds where others had failed and wins the girl. In *Culhwch and Olwen* this theme is triggered off by the motif of the Jealous Stepmother, which is itself fitted into an abbreviated but traditional account of the birth, upbringing and initiation of the hero. Culhwch declines to marry the daughter of his stepmother, whereupon the latter swears that he shall never lie with woman until he wins Olwen daughter of Ysbaddaden Chief Giant. Like Cú Chulainn making his way to the court of king Conchobor at Emain Macha, so Culhwch sets out for the court of king Arthur, but once entry is obtained to the royal circle — and this is never without difficulty in the conventional formula — their histories diverge: whereas Cú Chulainn proceeds through the several stages and trials culminating in his accession to the heroic society, in Culhwch's case this normal sequence is replaced by the quest for the giant's daughter which constitutes the body of the tale.

The essential pattern of this major section is simple, comprising quest, acquisition of magic helpers, imposition of tasks, and finally their fulfilment and the ensuing marriage, but in *Culhwch and Olwen* the author uses this as a convenient frame within which he has gathered a fascinating variety of tales as well as of references to miscellaneous traditions which often are poorly attested elsewhere or not at all. The containing structure is quite rigid, but within it there is considerable flexibility and endless scope for extension. Thus there are six helpers who set out on the initial search for Olwen, but others turn up in a vast list of the warriors of Arthur's court, characters such as Clust son of Clustfeinad 'Ear son of Hearer' — *were he to be buried seven fathoms in the earth, he would hear an ant fifty miles off when it stirred from its couch of a morning'* — or Medyr son of Medredydd 'Aim son of Aimer' — *who from Celli Wig* [in Cornwall] *would hit a wren on Esgeir Oerfel in Ireland, exactly through its two legs.* In this massive roll-call of Arthur's court the author ranges far and wide throughout the reaches of Welsh tradition, both written and oral, borrows a few prominent characters from Irish literature, and also includes a list of the ladies of the court. Even in the reading of it one is overwhelmed and captivated by the sheer exuberance of this spilling of resounding and intriguing names, some of them with flitters of story still attached, and one can imagine how effective such a cascade of sound and connotation must have been in oral recitation.

For this is one of the essential differences between the authors of the Four Branches and *Culhwch and Olwen*: one creating a simple but subtle style that depends for its effect as much on the eye as on the ear, the other joyfully accepting the forms of oral narration and adapting them freely and, to my mind, successfully to the written text. The catalogue of heroic and mythic names is a familiar device in Irish literature (including, in this instance, James Joyce's *Ulysses*), where, as in *Culhwch and Olwen*, it was obviously taken from the oral tradition, but nowhere is it used with the same boundless prodigality as in this instance. Oral storytellers knew well the accumulative force of repetition, whether it be straight repetition, or incremental repetition or the quasi-repetition of lists of famous people or places or things, and the author of *Culhwch and Olwen*, who clearly was familiar with oral poetry and storytelling, not merely makes use of the device, but constructs the greater part of his composition around it.[40]

First there is the list of Arthur's retinue, then the catalogue of the tasks, each introduced with the same verbal formula, and finally the serial account of their accomplishment (not to mention minor series such as the groups of warriors slain by the Twrch Trwyth). It conforms to the linear structure typical of Celtic literature and it has the great advantage that it can be extended more or less at will; but conversely, for the oral storyteller, and even for the medieval scribe, it is very much subject to the vagaries of memory. In our text the series of tasks is aptly divided into those required to provide the wedding feast and those required to comb and shave Ysbaddaden's hair for that occasion, but it has many inconsistencies: just over half of the tasks set are actually accomplished and they are not in the same order and some of them not in quite the same form as enunciated by Ysbaddaden. Some of them are passed over summarily, perhaps with the intention of expanding them where possible at some later time, but several provide the occasion for a fairly extensive narrative which must formerly have existed independently. For instance, the search for Mabon son of Modron who had been stolen from his mother when three days old embodies a valuable fragment of the mythology of one of the principal British deities. Contained within it is the preliminary quest for Eidoel son of Aer, which W. J. Gruffydd has argued plausibly is a doublet of the Mabon tale, and also a version of the international tale of the Oldest Animals compounded with two separate folk motifs: in this instance Cei and Gwrhyr Interpreter of Tongues seek knowledge of Mabon's whereabouts from the blackbird of Cilgwri, the stag of Rhedynfre, the owl of Cwm Cawlwyd and the eagle of Gwernabwy, all of them of phenomenal age, but their enquiries are fruitless until they come to the salmon of Llyn Llyw, who tells them where Mabon is in captivity and aids them in his rescue.

Most of the tales have their roots deep in mythology. Prominent British deities feature in the tale which tells of the conflict between Gwynn son of Nudd and Gwythyr son of Greidawl when Gwynn abducted Gwythyr's wife, Creiddylad daughter of Lludd Silverhand. By Arthur's intervention it was decided that the two should fight for her on every May Day till the Day of Judgement and that he who should win then should have possession of her. Another tells of the quest for the cauldron of Diwrnach the Irishman which is required to boil the meat for the wedding guests. When it is refused to Arthur's messengers, he takes his followers to Ireland in his ship *Prydwen* and seizes the cauldron by main force. This is clearly a derivative of Arthur's expedition to the Otherworld as told in the early poem *Preiddau Annwn* and a cognate of that recounted in *Branwen*. The most important single episode is that of the hunting of the great boar called Twrch Trwyth, between whose ears were the comb and shears without which the giant Ysbaddaden's hair could not be dressed for the wedding:

*And then Arthur gathered together what warriors there were in the Island of Britain and its three adjacent islands, and what there were in France and Brittany and Normandy and the Summer Country, and what there were of picked dogs and horses of renown. And with all those hosts he went to Ireland, and at his coming there was a great fear and trembling in Ireland . . .*

a passage which, in the Welsh, is as good an example as any of the author's command of a clear and finely modulated prose:

*Ac yna y Kynnullwys Arthur a oed o gynifywr yn teir ynys*
*Prydein ae their rac ynys, ac a oed yn Freinc a Llydaw a*
*Normandi a Gwlad yr Haf, ac a oed o gicwr dethol a march*
*clotuawr, ac y daeth ar niueroed hynny oll hyt yn Iwerdon, ac y*
*bu ouyn mawr ac ergryn racdaw yn Iwerdon.*

Following on this impressive muster they fight the
Twrch Trwyth and pursue him from Ireland to south
Wales and then at break-neck speed from one place to
another in the kind of circumambulation that gave
unlimited scope to the topographical and onomastic
expertise of the medieval storyteller, until finally the
implements are recovered from between his ears and
he disappears into the sea off Cornwall. The whole
story has a doublet in an earlier and much more
succinct episode about the killing of Ysgithyrwyn
Chief Boar whose tusk is needed to shave
Ysbaddaden, and the probability is that we have to do
with two variants of the same tradition. Both derive
from a basic theme which is well attested also in Irish
literature and which tells of the metamorphosis of
kings and princes into the form of fierce, malevolent
pigs who are hunted by a famous warrior.

The author has an eye for a good story and a fine sense
of narrative. We saw how he skilfully incorporated the
motif of the Oldest Animals into the quest for Mabon.
Another example of a folklore motif used with a
storyteller's flair is that of the helping ants. In some
versions of the international folktale which provides
the central plot of *Culhwch and Olwen* the hero is aided
not only by men but by animals whom he has
succoured in some way, and in many instances from
Europe and Asia this role is assigned to grateful ants.
In the Welsh tale Ysbaddaden points out where he
once sowed eighteen bushels of flax seed which did

not sprout. These, he demands, must be recovered within a single day and then re-sown to produce a veil for Olwen on her wedding day. Now it so happened that Gwythyr son of Greidawl had once come upon a blazing anthill and saved the community of ants within it, and these now returned his kindness by gathering in all the flax seed — but for a single one, and this was brought in before night by an ant that was lame.

The tale of *Culhwch and Olwen* has one obvious structural defect: in the folktale theme on which it is based the tasks are imposed in order to bring about the hero's death, but here Culhwch drops out of sight while the tasks are performed by Arthur and his men, reappearing only at the final denouement to take Olwen for his bride; consequently the narrative which started off as the heroic biography of Culhwch suddenly turns into an extension of the heroic cycle of Arthur. One may suggest various complicated reasons for this, but the simplest, and probably the most accurate, is that our author adopted the international theme of the giant's daughter, not for its own sake, but simply as a convenient frame within which he could accommodate a virtually unlimited miscellany of Welsh legend and heroic tradition, and that already by the eleventh century, when *Culhwch and Olwen* may have been composed, Arthur had begun to dominate the whole range of popular narrative, just as Fionn mac Cumhaill and his *fiana* were doing in Ireland around about the same time. The hunting of the Twrch Trwyth is already associated with Arthur in the catalogue of the Marvels of Britain in Nennius's ninth-century HISTORIA BRITTONUM, several other exploits in *Culhwch and Olwen* (for instance the raid on the Otherworld or Ireland and the killing of the Black

Witch) are credited to him in other earlier sources, and those which were not originally his exemplify the accretion of legend around his name which seems to have proceeded steadily from about the ninth century onwards.

It is true, none the less, that there is a structural dichotomy in *Culhwch and Olwen*; and yet the whole thing is carried off with such verve and panache that I doubt very much whether it seriously affects the modern reader's enjoyment of the tale (much less that of the medieval reader, or auditor). We moderns have perhaps a tendency to impose our own standards on medieval literary works that are still semi-oral in their composition and their performance and perhaps to set too great a stress on structural consistency as opposed to narrative validity. At the risk of appearing frivolous or irrelevant, I am tempted to apply to *Culhwch and Olwen* what a modern critic has written of Proust's À LA RECHERCHE DU TEMPS PERDU:

*The beginning and the end of the novel are firmly in place, the former leading us into and the latter out of the narrative. In between comes a malleable and infinitely expandable section, which did in fact more than triple its original size. This vast median segment has the resilience of life itself. No incident seems absolutely essential; all are significant when related to the rest. The opening and the close establish beyond challenge an overarching movement that encompasses all digressions and meanderings.*

*Mutatis mutandis* it is not wholly inappropriate.

One of the things we noted in the Four Branches was the quality of the dialogue: its ease and naturalness and the way in which it was attuned to the interplay of personalities. In this respect *Culhwch and Olwen* cannot compete, nor, one suspects, would its author have wished to do so. To have attempted the realistic humanism of Manawydan would have been quite foreign to his purpose, nor would it have served it much better to have cast his 'heroine' Olwen as an imperious and sharp-tongued goddess in mufti like Rhiannon or Aranrhod rather than the beautiful and passive prize of heroic endeavour that the wonder tale requires. Olwen has more in common with Branwen than a rhyming name; they are more or less in the same mould, and the only essential difference between them is that Olwen's story has a happy ending. Consequently if the dialogue in *Culhwch and Olwen* is more conventional and less personal than that in the Four Branches, this may be less a reflection on its author's literary ability than a measure of the disparity between two genres of composition.

For there can be no question about his mastery of Welsh prose. His writing is not perhaps as finely wrought as that of the Four Branches, but it is more varied in its pace and style, and if one were seeking a conspectus of Welsh prose styles undoubtedly his would be the more fruitful source. He had a comprehensive knowledge of traditional literature — hardly a passage in his work but evokes analogies within extant Welsh texts or analogies in Irish which no longer have any attested counterparts in Welsh — and not merely does he imitate the matter of his sources, but he also echoes their style. For general narrative purposes he has a prose that is clean, fluent and functional, but which can quickly change pace to produce a breathless gallop as in parts of the Twrch Trwyth chase. It contains a number of older words not found in the rest of Middle Welsh prose, which may indicate on the one hand that the text is older than the others and, on the other, that the author was more familiar with early sources. He has also more sonorous, declamatory styles that have their origin in oral narration. Some of these, like the high-flown account of Culhwch's progress to Arthur's court, are in the nature of set pieces where the storyteller could give free rein to his eloquence; they are extremely frequent in Irish literature, where a strange hero, or group of heroes, is observed approaching, and generally make use of the same kinds of linguistic embellishment, such as alliteration, a more or less exotic vocabulary, and series of verbless sentences or sentences composed of a noun followed by a relative clause. In this particular instance the description of Culhwch leads up to his encounter with Glewlwyd the porter who seeks to prevent him from entering Arthur's court, an episode which has a close analogue in an early Arthurian poem in the Black Book of Carmarthen and another in Irish in the famous account of the youthful god Lugh's arrival at Tara. And still within the same episode, when Glewlwyd goes inside to consult Arthur about this persistent newcomer, he ventilates his perplexed wonder in terms which obviously follow a traditional pattern:

'Have you news from the gate?' said Arthur. 'I have. Two thirds of my life are past, and two thirds of yours. I was of old in Caer Se and Asse, in Sach and Salach, in Lotor and Ffotor. I was of old in India the Great and India the Lesser. I was of old in the contest between the two Ynyrs, when the twelve hostages were brought from Llychlyn. And of old I was in Egrop, and in Africa was I, and in the islands of Corsica, and in Caer Brythwch and Brythach, and Nerthach. I was there of old when you slew the war-band of Gleis son of Merin, when you slew Mil the Black, son of Dugum; I was there of old in Caer Oeth and Anoeth, and in Caer Nefenhyr

*Nine-teeth. Fair kingly men we saw there, but never did I see a man so comely as this who is even now at the entrance to the gate.'*

This catalogue of far-flung exploits belongs to a familiar type in Celtic literature, but here the author has turned it into a splendidly sustained and extravagant build-up for his comment on Culhwch, drawing maximum effect from the spaced repetition of the phrase *Mi a uum gynt* 'I was of old' (where, incidentally, the serial use of the first person preterite verb does not lack precedents in early Welsh verse). His is indeed the art that conceals art, drawing freely upon the familiar and sometimes banal devices of traditional narrative, yet turning them deftly to his own artistic design. It has a touch of pastiche, as of a writer who views the commonplaces of tradition with a mixture of attachment and amusement, and in case the reader should be obtuse enough to miss this in the present instance, it is brought out clearly in the unconscious humour of Arthur's response to Glewlwyd:

*Said Arthur: 'If you came in walking, let you go out running . . . A shameful thing it is to leave in wind and rain a man such as you tell of.'*

Descriptions of idealized physical beauty are another speciality of the Celtic storyteller, and again the author of *Culhwch* is not found wanting. His account of Olwen is faithful to the traditional type in its dappled imagery and its beautifully cadenced phrases (in the Welsh), but it has a certain overplus which marks it clearly as his own creation, a lightness of touch and a delicate hyperbole which hovers between mythic truth and literary fantasy:

*She was sent for. And she came, with a robe of flame-red silk about her, and around the maiden's neck a torque of red gold, and precious pearls thereon and rubies. Yellower was her head than the flower of the broom, whiter was her flesh than the foam of the wave; whiter were her palms and her fingers than the shoots of the marsh trefoil from amidst the fine gravel of a welling spring. Neither the eye of the mewed hawk, nor the eye of the thrice-mewed falcon, not an eye was there fairer than hers. Whiter were her breasts than the breast of the white swan, redder were her cheeks than the reddest foxgloves. Whosoever beheld her would be filled with love of her. Four white trefoils sprang up behind her wherever she went; and for that reason was she called Olwen ('White-track').*

He is, one feels, himself captivated by the image he seeks to re-create in words, while fully aware that he is at the same time parodying the genre of which it is part. One assumes that the happy conceit which supplies the explanation of Olwen's name (and the name itself?) is of his invention; but I am surely not mistaken in thinking that he uses it to poke a little gentle fun at the art of onomastic etymology, which plays such a vast role in traditional literature.

This element of benevolent pastiche which I discern in *Culhwch* brings us into the ill-marked area between wit and humour where the unwary modern can so easily miss one or the other where it is present and imagine it where it is not. For instance, when Culhwch enters Arthur's hall the two heroes engage in grandiloquent exchanges culminating in Arthur's offer of a boon:

*Said Arthur, 'Though you bide not here, chieftain, you will obtain the boon your head and your tongue shall name, as far as wind dries, as far as rain wets, as far as sun runs, as far as sea stretches, as far as earth extends, save only my ship and my mantle, and Caledfwlch my sword, and Rhongomyniad my spear, and*

*Wynebgwrthucher my shield, and Carnwennan my dagger, and Gwenhwyfar my wife.'*

Is there, or is there not, a touch of dry humour in the juxtaposition of Arthur's (virtually) limitless magnanimity and the rather impressive list of reservations he attaches to it, as indeed in the position he assigns Gwenhwyfar? His caution seems almost legalistic in comparison with Pwyll's *naïveté* in rather similar circumstances, and if we are not sure whether the slyness is intended, then, coming from an author of such proven sensibility, the ambiguity probably is.

But most of the humour in *Culhwch* is anything but elusive, and there is enough of it present to make the author of the Four Branches seem a sourpuss by comparison. For example, when the wife of the monstrous shepherd Custennin comes to welcome Cei with an embrace, she compresses into a twisted withe the stake that he had providently thrust between her hands in lieu of his neck, whereupon he remarks, *'Woman, had it been I you squeezed in this fashion, there would have been no need for another to love me ever. An ill love, that!'* Or there is the disproportion between the seriousness of Ysbaddaden's wounds and the triviality of his complaints: when Culhwch strikes him in the ball of his eye so that it comes out through the nape of his neck, his immediate response is, *'You cursed savage son-in-law! So long as I am left alive, the sight of my eyes will be the worse. When I go against the wind they will water, a headache I shall have, and a giddiness each new moon . . . '* (which, translated to the idiom of early twentieth-century Albany, New York, would surely come very close indeed to the dry understatement of *Martin was right. A 22 in the eye gives you a hell of a headache* in William Kennedy's BILLY PHELAN'S

GREATEST GAME). Or the knock-about anti-heroics of the encounter with the Black Witch, when she administers an unmerciful drubbing to the several warriors who tackle her before Arthur. Here we have the typical boisterous humour that has been a staple element of Celtic oral narrative throughout the ages and which in more recent times has crossed the linguistic boundaries into Anglo-Irish and Anglo-Welsh storytelling.

More than anything else, I feel, it is this capacity to reproduce the richness, the variety and the sheer vitality of oral storytelling that gives *Culhwch and Olwen* its special attraction. It is a veritable cornucopia where every passing name or reference may be a signpost to a hidden tale or to a whole area of forgotten tradition and where a great many of the genres of oral narrative and their special styles and techniques are re-created with complete mastery and authenticity, but at the same time with a touch of detachment and humour that bespeaks a certain intellectual sophistication. If the whole work appears unpretentious in its conception, it is certainly not through lack of competence or dedication on the part of the author, but more likely because he does not take himself or his social function quite so seriously as does the author of the Four Branches. He shows none of the social or moral concern of the latter, except in so far as his general attitude may be reflected in the tone of his narrative. Like all tellers of heroic and wonder tales he is concerned with types rather than with personalities, but at the same time he is too sensitive a writer not to invest the words and actions of his stock characters with a certain emotional colour: even the monstrous Ysbaddaden evokes our sympathy and in the end appears more the victim than the villain of the whole

73

proceedings, an embryonic reversal of roles which tells something of the author's questioning approach to the inherited literary categories.

Judged by the strictest standards of structural unity his composition has obvious shortcomings, but these are more than redeemed by the sweep and vigour and teeming variety which hold the reader's unflagging interest from Culhwch's entrance to Ysbaddaden's exit. His primary aim, as he makes abundantly clear, is not to moralize or to educate but to entertain, and not merely has he achieved this beyond question, but in doing so he has given us a more comprehensive view of the forms and resources of Welsh literary tradition than can be found in any other medieval text.

# The three minor tales

The tragedy of oral art is that it cannot normally survive cultural change unless, paradoxically, it has been recorded in written form. We are almost entirely ignorant of early Welsh music and song, though they were an essential part of the living *performance* of oral literature, and no doubt we should be equally blind to the rich variety of the literature itself were it not for the many allusions in the later poetry and triads which crowd our imagination with tantalizing glimpses of unrecorded myth and legend. What survives in manuscript covers only a small part of the oral tales of the early period; that much is certain. But why these particular items of tradition should have been elected to permanence rather than so many others is something we can only conjecture. In the case of the Four Branches and *Culhwch and Olwen* we have seen individual authors at work shaping their own texts from the materials, mainly oral, which they had at their disposal. Both are eclectic, but the author of *Culhwch and Olwen* works within the self-imposed limits of the framework tale of the quest and marriage of the giant's daughter, while the author of the Four Branches has made a more arbitrary selection in the sense that he is less concerned with the integrity and interrelationship of his materials within the living tradition than with their usefulness in his personal composition. The three romances are perhaps a more characteristic product of their age in that they reflect something of the medieval notion of courtly society and the increasing vogue of Arthurian legend.

Similarly, of the three minor tales two, *The Dream of Maxen Wledig* and *Lludd and Llefelys*, belong to the genre of traditional history which had always been an important part of the professional repertoire of the learned poet and it is reasonable to assume that their writing down (as opposed to their composition) was one of the products of the twelfth-century pseudo-historical movement dominated by Geoffrey of Monmouth.

The story of Lludd and Llefelys was inserted into one of the earliest of the Welsh versions of Geoffrey's HISTORY OF THE KINGS OF BRITAIN and occurs regularly in subsequent versions of the Welsh text. It was taken up in this form by some author, probably an ecclesiastic, who expanded it and partly rewrote it to produce the independent text which goes by the name of *Cyfranc Lludd a Llefelys* 'The Story of Lludd and Llefelys'. But, while the extant tale seems thus to derive directly from the Welsh translation of the HISTORY, it did not originate there, for there are clear indications that a version was already current, probably in oral form, during the eleventh century.[41] The narrative is short and prosaic and its interest is historical and thematic rather than literary. It tells of three banes or oppressions which afflicted the Island of Britain during the reign of Lludd son of Beli Mawr and how these were removed through the counsel of Lludd's brother Llefelys. The first of these oppressions was a people called the Coraniaid whose hearing and knowledge were such that nothing could be said throughout the land without their knowing it, the second a scream that was heard every May-eve and which left women and animals barren and men without vigour, and the third a mighty man of magic power who caused everyone to fall asleep by his enchantment and carried off all the food and drink from the king's courts.

These three afflictions have many analogies elsewhere in Celtic literature, and basically they are all concerned with the disturbance of human society and its affairs through the interference of preternatural powers, but they are here also brought into connection with traditional and learned concepts of British history. The baneful cry of the second affliction is explained as that of a dragon — a decent British dragon it would seem — which is engaged in desperate conflict with a foreign dragon, and Llefelys gives precise instructions as to how they are to be found, soused in mead, and then buried in the strongest place in the land. In this way it is designed to link up with the ninth-century account by Nennius of the building of Vortigern's fortress in Snowdonia and the uncovering of the two dragons, the red and the white, which represented the British and the Saxons and prefigured the defeat of the invaders. In fact the whole tale of *Lludd and Llefelys* has been described by Dr Rachel Bromwich as an expansion of an extant historical, or pseudo-historical, triad which tells of three of the invasions of Britain: the Coraniaid, the Picts and the Saxons.[42] In native secular tradition there had never been any clear or consistent distinction between myth and history, and even when the division had been introduced by the Latin-orientated scholars of the monasteries it was always prone to break down under the pressure of the mythopoeic view of the past. In Ireland the historical Vikings tended to be assimilated in the popular mind to the mythical invaders known as Fomhoire, or Fomorians, and it may well be that the Coraniaid played a similar role in oral Welsh tradition to that of the Fomhoire in Irish. It may even be that they were

77

once the sole or the central oppression in the original mythic narrative from which the extant text is derived: Lludd occurs elsewhere as Lludd Llaw Ereint 'Lludd of the Silver Hand, or Arm', and his obvious counterpart in Irish is the divine Nuadha Airgedlámh, who corresponds to him in name and epithet and whose kingdom is saved from the Fomhoire by the intervention of the god Lugh, just as Lludd's kingdom is saved by the intervention of Llefelys.

But whatever imaginative quality the original myth may have possessed, little of it has filtered through into the extant tale. Stylistically it has some of the characteristic defects of Middle Welsh translation prose: rather dull and ponderous, it lacks on the one hand the urbane fluency of the Four Branches and on the other the colour and vivacity of *Culhwch and Olwen*.

Fortunately this pedantic style is exceptional in *The Mabinogi* and is certainly not a feature of the *The Dream of Maxen Wledig*. Essentially this is a lyrical short story composed on a single narrative motif. Its hero Maxen is in origin the historical Magnus Maximus who was elected emperor by his troops in Britain in AD 383 and who prosecuted his cause on the continent until slain by Theodosius in 388. Its heroine is Elen Luyddawg who seems to be an amalgam of a native goddess figure with the well-known St Helena, mother of Constantine the Great. Maxen became a figure of consequence in Welsh tradition: his departure with his troops left Britain open to the attacks of Picts, Scots and Saxons and at some stage his impact on British history was magnified by ingeniously equating his troops with the insular colonizers of Brittany and by casting him as the ancestor of several early Welsh dynasties. Elen, like many Celtic goddesses, seems to have been regarded as a divine ancestress and some Welsh redactor or storyteller had the happy thought of linking the two through the familiar motif of the love-dream.

According to the tale Macsen, emperor of Rome, was abroad hunting one day and lay down to rest, and while he slept he had a dream and in his dream he travelled by land and sea to a distant country where eventually he came to a splendid castle, richly adorned with gold and glittering stones, and in that castle sat a maiden of extraordinary beauty dressed in silks and rich brocades. The maiden rose to greet him, he embraced her, and they sat together on a chair of gold with his cheek against hers. But at that moment Maxen was awakened from his sleep by the sounds of his hounds and horses, and the castle and the maiden vanished from his view, leaving him helpless and wearied and consumed by love. For a full year his messengers journeyed throughout the world seeking the woman of his vision but found no tidings of her, and it was then it was suggested — in the best tradition of the detective story — that the initial circumstances of Maxen's visionary pilgrimage should be re-enacted. This was done. The emperor went hunting as before and, from the point at which he had experienced his vision, messengers went forth and retraced his route to the distant castle of Caernarfon. On their return to Rome they reported to the emperor and he in turn set out to follow in person the road he had formerly travelled in spirit.

The short story of Maxen's love for Elen ends effectively at this point, but, in a way that is familiar from written Irish narrative, the redactor prolongs his

79

text with several items of antiquarian interest — the explanation of place-names, the origin of the Roman roads traditionally associated with Elen, and the settlement of Brittany — the main purpose of which was no doubt to 'document' his narrative, in other words to authenticate it by appealing to the palpable facts of the contemporary environment. This kind of specious validation is a familiar feature of pre-modern thought and has been invoked by learned storytellers throughout the world, not least among the Celts. In early Irish literature it is commonplace, and if to the modern reader it often seems to mar a good tale, it must be remembered that in the traditional concept of historical narrative as it obtained in early Wales and Ireland fiction in the absolute modern sense had little meaning or reality and that a historical tale, even when composed as entertainment or political propaganda, could hardly avoid being treated in one way or another as a historical document. Such was the sense of cultural continuity that all composition in the inherited modes tended to be assimilated to the greater unity of tradition and when a tale was told it was natural for the storyteller to corroborate its authenticity by reference to observable reality, as when a medieval Irish storyteller closes his narrative by citing one or more actual place-names which derive from it (though our more pedantic science can often show that the causation operated in the reverse direction!). It is true that among the tales of *The Mabinogi* — and I have noted it particularly in the case of the Four Branches — we find a more modern and sophisticated approach to the composition of prose narrative and one need not assume that the author of *The Dream of Maxen* believed the story he told of the marriage of Maxen and Elen; yet the inherited moulds of thought and expression are not easily broken, and even where the sacred 'history' of the tribe or nation seems to have become the stuff of secular and self-conscious literature and the teller of tales their emancipated author, still the weight of time-old usage acts as a powerful brake on arbitrary innovation.

The fact remains that the antiquarian tail-piece impairs the artistic unity of the text, and this is the more noticeable against the consummate craftsmanship of the main narrative. The structure is of the simplest — introduction, the triple journey, first by Maxen in his dream, secondly by the searchers and thirdly by Maxen in the flesh, and finally the union of the lovers — but it is handled with a quite remarkable skill and fluency. In the dream the journey is described in considerable detail and with much stylistic elaboration, during the search it is recounted more concisely, though this time the destination is firmly identified by the use of place-names, and in the final instance it is compressed to a couple of sentences, reflecting Maxen's impatience to reach his goal, but to the place-names of the second journey are now added the names of Elen's father and brothers; in other words the reiteration is marked simultaneously by decreasing volume and increasing definition, thus providing a kind of enriching counterpoint to the whole narrative. The increasing succinctness and definition of the prose crystallizes the growing reality of the incidents, the environment and the characters, from the timeless world of the dream to the finite precinct of Arfon and Anglesey and Eryri.

The co-ordination of sense and style is particularly notable in the dream sequence: the sentences are more varied and more sinuous than in the later sections, the narrative more leisurely, as befits the infinite, untrammelled world of the vision. But what is perhaps still more remarkable is the way in which the author has used the verb 'to see', which in early Irish and Welsh frequently connoted the preternatural vision of the seer: in this one section of the narrative he employs the imperfect indicative *gwelei* 'saw, could see' twenty-four times, not to mention five instances of the pluperfect *gwelsei*, so that the whole sequence is dominated by the sense of vision in both its natural and supernatural forms. Yet such is the rhythm and balance of his prose that this constant repetition never appears laboured or monotonous. And finally the triad of journeys is bound together by a simple verbal echo which is probably intentional (though with a writer of talent or genius one is not always certain whether the effects he achieves come about by accident or by design): when Maxen encountered Elen at the end of his dream journey, *he threw his arms around the maiden's neck*, only to be frustrated by the ending of his dream, and again when he eventually recovered her in reality *the emperor threw his arms around her neck. And that night he slept with her.* This verbal reprise forms a nexus with the dream sequence, so that Maxen's quest for Elen appears to resume and find its consummation precisely where previously it was interrupted.

Celtic literature, and particularly Irish literature, has many instances of the love-dream or vision, and generally *The Dream of Maxen Wledig* has been associated with this traditional genre. More recently, however, it has been suggested that its affinities are rather with a well-attested eastern or Indian variant of the love-dream which had migrated westwards.[43] The argument is cogently presented and may indeed well be true, though I confess that I am not yet entirely persuaded of this. In any event, our concern with the tale is more immediate, and we can afford to suspend judgement on the question of ultimate origins while admiring the exceptional artistry of its composition.

*The Dream of Maxen Wledig* is 'literary' — as indeed are all the tales we have been examining — in the sense that, while it draws more or less freely on the stuff of traditional oral narrative, it has evidently been composed in terms of the written text. But when Dr Thomas Parry speaks of that other dream-tale, *Breuddwyd Rhonabwy* 'The Dream of Rhonabwy', as *the most literary of them all*, he means something more than this. What he appears to be saying is that its author consciously places himself outside — or above — native literary tradition in a way that our other authors do not. Where the rest — even the urbane author of the Four Branches — display a certain ambivalence to the traditional matter of their narratives, affecting to believe in them as myth or history even when there is evidence that they do not, the author of *The Dream of Rhonabwy* keeps his tongue firmly and visibly in his cheek from beginning to end. His work is a prolonged parody of native genres and styles — the kind of thing we found already in *Culhwch and Olwen*, except that there it was used incidentally and without endangering the authenticity of the general narrative while here it constitutes the very substance and *raison d'être* of the composition.

The satire is not confined to the dream which forms the main body of the tale; it begins already with the first line of the prologue: *Madawg son of Maredudd held Powys from end to end, that is, from Porffordd unto Gwafan in the uplands of Arwystli* . . . This is the conventional form of opening for traditional king-tales, in Irish as well as in Welsh, and its use here promises a kind of narrative quite different to what follows, thus introducing from the very outset the discrepancy between form and reality, between implication and intent, which lies at the heart of literary irony and satire. Incidentally, since Madog ap Maredudd died in 1159 the reference to him is a clue to the date of the tale; unfortunately, like many such clues, its usefulness depends upon our being able to interpret it correctly, or at least incontrovertibly. Some scholars have assigned the composition of the text to the thirteenth century on the grounds that Madog's name would hardly have been used in story until some considerable time after his death, others would date it within or shortly after his lifetime on the grounds that he was not outstanding enough to be mentioned very long after his death. The matter is not made any simpler by the parodic-satirical vein in which the story is written. For instance, in this connection T. M. Charles-Edwards invokes a passage in the tale where Rhonabwy and his companions are brought before Arthur by Iddawg Cordd Prydain:

'May God bless you,' said Arthur. 'Where, Iddawg, did you find those little men?'
'I found them further along the road.'
The emperor then smiled wryly.
'Lord', said Iddawg, 'what are you laughing at?'
'Iddawg', said Arthur, 'I am not laughing, but it seems sad to me that men as insignificant as these should be guarding this island after men as fine as those that guarded it of yore.'

He makes the very acute point that if this is satire aimed at contemporaries its relevance depends on their being contemporaries, and so he would support the earlier dating.[44] Most probably he is right, provided one can be satisfied that the author is in fact satirizing the men of Powys in the twelfth century. But *The Dream of Rhonabwy* has strong elements of parody throughout and it may be that in this instance the author is simply parodying the tendency to elevate the heroes of old to giant stature by comparison with contemporary men. In the long Irish frame-story called *Acallam na Senórach* 'The Colloquy of the Old Men', which was composed in the same period as *The Dream of Rhonabwy*, the same motif occurs: when Caílte and his fellow-survivors from the heroic fraternity of the *fiana* first came to St Patrick and his clerics, we are told that *fear fell upon them before the tall men with their huge wolf-hounds that accompanied them, for they were not people of one epoch or of one time with the clergy*. Fionn and his *fiana* are often represented as giants in modern Irish oral tradition, but this is not the case in medieval written texts and the suggestion has been that where this motif occurs in *Acallam na Senórach* it is due to the influence of unlearned oral tradition. Given then the many long-standing analogies between Fionn and his *fiana* on the one hand and Arthur and his troops on the other, one may perhaps reasonably assume that the latter were also credited with gigantic stature in popular tradition and the motif is not of the author's invention in the story of Rhonabwy's dream. Nor need his use of it be satirical; it may be nothing more than harmless parody.

In this regard it is worth noting that certain stylistic elements which are part of the normal dramatic rhetoric of learned and popular medieval narrative may be highlighted or parodied simply by using them in a satiric or humorous context. There are many instances of this in *The Dream of Rhonabwy*, but one is particularly apposite at this point because, like the abnormal stature of Arthur and his men, it seems likely to have derived from popular storytelling. When Rhonabwy and his companions first saw Iddawg Cordd Prydain riding towards them they took fright and tried to flee, but he pursued them *and when his horse breathed forth his breath they drew away from him, and when it breathed in they drew near to him, right up to the horse's chest.* This has analogues in modern Irish story-telling. Professor Delargy quotes one from a tale which he recorded in 1933 in Co. Galway:

*The giant fell asleep. The first snore he made he brought Sir Slanders, his nephew, to the uvula at the back of his throat, and when he breathed out again, he sent him flying up to the rafters. Sir Slanders spent the night like that between the back of the giant's throat and the top beam of the rafters in the castle.*[45]

In this instance the Irish folk variant has more sheer vitality than the medieval Welsh. It exploits the burlesque in a way that is characteristic of the traditional wonder tale, but which would not blend with the more polished style of the Rhonabwy tale. What lends the motif its artistic nuance in the Welsh composition is the fact that it is set within a web of sustained parody, and no doubt its medieval readers, or auditors, being more familiar than we can ever be with the staple elements of popular oral narrative, would have been alive to the significance of its use in such a context.

The fact is that *The Dream of Rhonabwy* is not a story in the sense that the other texts of *The Mabinogi* are stories, nor can it have been conceived as such (the virtual absence of female characters underlines this fact). It does not tell a tale, but rather creates a situation comprising several sustained images. It uses some of the technical and stylistic devices of oral narrative, but it has no 'plot' worth mentioning, no real progression of incident and none but the most inconclusive of endings. This is how it goes, in brief summary:

*Madog son of Maredudd, ruler of Powys, sent men to seek out his renegade brother Iorwerth, who had gone raiding in England. Among them is Rhonabwy (who, untypically, is given no epithet or patronymic). With two companions he found lodgings, if not hospitality, in a house of extreme dirt and squalor which is described in convincing detail. Lying on a yellow ox-hide he dreamed that he and his companions were approaching the River Severn when they were overtaken by Iddawg Cordd Prydain. Proceeding onwards they came to where Arthur was sitting on an island in the middle of the river and it was at this point that he remarked on the insignificant stature of Rhonabwy and his companions. Meanwhile two troops, one as red as blood, the other arrayed in black and white, came and pitched their tents nearby. An oncoming rider spurred his horse into the ford and splashed Arthur and Bishop Bedwin who was with him so that they were 'as wet as if they had been dragged out of the river'. Another warrior, Caradawg Freichfras, reminded Arthur that he had promised to be at the battle of Baddon by noon to fight against Osla Big-knife, and the emperor (as Arthur is titled in this text) got his troops on the move forthwith. There is an account of the advance of the men of Llychlyn (Scandinavia) and Denmark led by March son of Meirchiawn and Edern son of Nudd respectively; the high-flown description of their dress and accoutrements, brilliant white for the men of Llychlyn and pure black for the others, is constructed out of the old terminology found in the annals and elsewhere, both in Wales and in Ireland, which distinguishes between the white and black heathens of the north. Evidently the battle was then joined at Baddon, but there is no actual account of the fighting. What follows instead is a series of several rather flamboyant picture-pieces: Cei performing equestrian pyrotechnics in the midst of Arthur's forces, Cadwr Earl of Cornwall presenting Arthur's sword to him, Eiryn Wych spreading Arthur's mantle of brocaded silk on the ground and*

87

*setting his golden throne upon it, and finally Arthur playing*
gwyddbwyll *(a board-game) with Owain son of Urien in a richly*
*drawn sequence whose relevance is hardly obvious but which*
*nevertheless takes up almost half the text. While they were*
*playing, word was brought a first, a second and a third time that*
*Arthur's men were attacking Owain's ravens, but Arthur ignored*
*all Owain's appeals to restrain them. Then Owain ordered his*
*standard to be raised and immediately his ravens set about killing*
*and maiming the emperor's men. He in his turn was unmoved by*
*Arthur's pleas to call off his ravens and it was only when Arthur*
*crushed all the pieces on the playing board that he ordered his*
*standard to be lowered and peace restored. Just then four-and-*
*twenty horsemen came from Osla to ask a truce of Arthur. Bards*
*came to sing Arthur's praises in terms that were intelligible only*
*to themselves and were rewarded with gold and silver brought as*
*a tribute to Arthur from the Isles of Greece. The story ends with*
*Rhonabwy being awakened by the commotion after a sleep that*
*had lasted for three days and three nights.*

It seems inconceivable that such a disjointed yet
closely wrought text could have been intended for oral
recital; its whole value depends not on its narrative
but on the sophistication of its style and nuance, and
this could only have been appreciated by a reader, an
informed reader. In a brief apologue to the text we are
told that

*neither bard nor storyteller knows the Dream without a book —*
*by reason of the number of colours that were on the horses, and all*
*that variety of rare colours both on the arms and their trappings,*
*and on the precious mantles, and the magic stones,*

but the fact is that, while the text contains much
colourful description, neither its language nor its
diction is particularly abstruse, and I suspect that the
author is simply poking some good-humoured fun at
the pretensions of traditional storytellers while

indirectly acknowledging the fact that *The Dream* was a written text intended to be read.

This would be in keeping with the whole spirit and execution of *The Dream*. It is parody rather than satire, and, as such, it would be unwise to look in it for serious historical comment. We saw that Arthur's disparaging comment on the puny stature of Rhonabwy and his companions is perhaps less a conscious reflection on contemporary society or personages than a play on a familiar motif of popular narrative. Similarly, when the author describes with the same dramatic detail the meanness and squalor of Rhonabwy's lodgings and later the richness and splendour of Arthur's retinue, one cannot assume — as has been done — that he sees himself seriously in the role of *laudator temporis acti*, eulogist of the glories of the past. The contrast between past and present is drawn with style and vigour, but also with an element of conscious hyperbole that smacks of parody, and this impression is confirmed by a number of flaws which the author has sewn carefully into his account of the magnificence of Arthur the battle-leader and of his bizarre behaviour during the absurdly protracted episode of the board-game. If this has any purpose, surely it is to puncture the pretensions of the conventional *laudator temporis acti*.

There is scarcely a single passage in the text which cannot be read as parody, and this extends to the author's choice of the dream as the thematic frame of his narrative. The mantic dream was a familiar feature of Celtic ritual: it is well attested in Irish literature and even down to the seventeenth or eighteenth century Irish and Scottish poets continued to simulate the practice of the seer by composing their verse while lying on their beds in utter darkness. In at least one Irish account the seers seeking revelation are said to lie on the hides of bulls which had been sacrificed, and it is clear that Rhonabwy's vision and that of the Irish poet-seers relate to the same sacred procedure for acquiring hidden knowledge: for all one knows (and one knows remarkably little of these matters), it may be that the learned Welsh poets of medieval Wales continued to imitate the ancient usage as did their opposites in Ireland. But in one respect the author of our text gives a significant twist to the function of the dream: where traditionally it was invoked to gain prescience of future events, he uses it as a device for recovering a vision of the distant past, and he further underlines his irreverent treatment of the theme by making it a casual rather than a calculated occurrence and by substituting for the solemn ambience of the rite the flea-ravaged squalor of Rhonabwy's lodgings.

But he does not always signal his intent by such a note of near-burlesque. More often he has resort to a trick which has been part of the repertoire of the humorous writer or raconteur throughout the ages: the use of unmotivated digression and detail. The long episode of the board-game and Owain's ravens is written with such extreme precision and sense of style that it should clearly have some profound significance, but one looks for this in vain and in the end one is compelled inevitably to the conclusion that it is nothing more than an elaborate deception of the reader's expectations, a parody of the dramatic, descriptive set-pieces of traditional narrative, in short a witty and elegant literary spoof.

Characters pop in and out without evident motivation. Owain son of Urien is introduced casually as if he had already been part of the narrative, which he has not. Generally they are introduced with much descriptive detail, in the manner of traditional narrative, and are then identified by Iddawg in response to Rhonabwy's query, but, taken severally, they are narrative culs-de-sac contributing little to the advancement of the story, such as it is, and in point of fact it is — with the exception of the game between Arthur and Owain — little more than the sum of these dramatis personae in search of a drama. This is in a sense the whole point of the author's *jeu d'esprit*: to create a setting and assemble the cast for a story that never materializes, and if the result is a narrative that is episodic and inconsequential and so often deflected from its probable route that it ends up going nowhere, this is precisely as the author intended it.

*The Dream of Rhonabwy* is a sustained exercise in parody, but its parody consists not so much in the distortion or exaggeration of its models as in their incongruous juxtaposition, and, as with all good parody, it is always at risk of being confused with the object of its irony. We have a nice example of this in Alfred Nutt's comment on *The Dream* in his notes to Lady Charlotte Guest's translation of *The Mabinogi*:

*No story that I know of is better fitted to exemplify the peculiar quality of the Celtic genius in literature. Much has been written of Celtic glamour, Celtic mysticism, Celtic natural magic. On the other hand, it has been pointed out that the especial characteristics of early Celtic romance are delight in pure and vivid colour, in elaborate and minutely detailed descriptions of form. Irreconcilable qualities, it has been said; one or the other set of assertions must be wrong. I think this story enables us to see that the alleged irreconcilability is only apparent. Never, perhaps, was the craft of miniature painting in letters carried out with such infinite perfection of formal detail, such pellucid purity of colour. And yet the effect of the whole is that of glamour, of natural magic in the highest degree. The map is drawn with the exquisite precision and minute detail of a fifteenth-century portulan, but the country depicted lies among 'perilous seas, a fairy land forlorn'.*

It is not that Nutt's remarks on the character of Celtic romance are incorrect, but rather that they are misdirected. The setting conjured up in *The Dream* is not the mystic, colourful, preternatural world of Celtic romance but the author's tongue-in-cheek version of it, and while parody may sometimes misfire by improving on its model it surely does not do so in this instance: the parodistic element is too dominant for that and the characteristic lyric sincerity of Celtic romance too obviously absent to permit of any lasting doubt. *The Dream of Rhonabwy* is a remarkable piece of literary virtuosity, but in its design and execution it lacks the inner dynamism of romantic commitment, or even the infectious vigour and enthusiasm of the great Irish parody of *The Vision of Mac Con Glinne*. Its brilliant if somewhat brittle craftsmanship compels our admiration, but it is too static, too intellectually controlled, to evoke our sympathetic participation.

# The three romances

With the three romances we move into the mainstream of European literary tradition. We now find ourselves in that world of the romantic imagination which was being explored from the middle of the twelfth century onwards by men such as Chrétien de Troyes, Hartmann von Aue and Gottfried von Strassburg and actively promoted and patronized by sophisticated secular rulers, among whom the most notable was Eleanor of Aquitaine in her court at Poitiers, 'the chief academy of Western Europe for teaching the arts of courtesy'. This idealized world of chivalry and romance derived much of its substance and inspiration from the tradition of Celtic Britain — the *matière de Bretagne* — and for many its focal point was the legendary court of Arthur of the Britons, source and touchstone of knightly honour. The insular legends of Arthur, which had proliferated in popular oral tradition from the eighth or ninth century onwards, were refined and systematized during the twelfth century by a series of historians, storytellers and *conteurs* — Welsh, Breton and French — swept the native *chansons de geste* from their primacy in France and subsequently spread on a wave of popularity throughout the countries of western Europe. In France itself they were peculiarly attuned to the mood and condition of a changing society which had experienced the idealism, however flawed, of the Crusades, a society, moreover, in which great lords amassed territories and vassals while at the same time many young and vigorous members of the cadet nobility

found themselves restless and landless and readily susceptible to the attractions of the new courtly mode of life which was enacted in reality at the court of Poitiers and which found its mythology, and to some extent its ideology, in the apparently inexhaustible resources of Arthurian legend with its blend of individual freedom and commitment. Through Eleanor of Aquitaine's marriage to Henry II the *roman courtois* and the courtly life in general became closely linked to the fortunes and aspirations of the Angevin Empire, which extended at one stage from Scotland to Toulouse and was the arbiter of French-speaking civilization in the twelfth century. This was the world to which Welsh vernacular tradition was partially assimilated in the matter and the style of the three romances.

The special role of the romances is clear on purely internal grounds, but it is further emphasized by the remarkable fact that they have more or less close counterparts among the works of Chrétien de Troyes: *Erec et Enide* corresponding to *Geraint Son of Erbin*, *Yvain (Le Chevalier au Lion)* to *Owain (The Lady of the Fountain)*, and *Perceval (Conte del Graal)* to *Peredur Son of Efrawg*. The degree of correspondence is such as to presuppose a close relationship between the two sets of narratives, but the precise nature of this relationship has still to be determined. One view that was once widely held assumed that the Welsh texts were derived from the French: this rested on the obvious evidence of continental influence in the Welsh texts and on the relatively late date sometimes assigned to them, but clearly there has been misinterpretation of the criteria in both instances and it now emerges from a close comparison of the texts that a theory of simple borrowing is untenable. An alternative theory

94

accepted the British origin of the French tales and assumed that the Welsh tales from which they derived were carried to France by Breton *conteurs* before 1100; the resulting French versions would have provided the common source for the extant texts in both languages. The difficulty with this theory, as R.M. Jones has pointed out,[46] is that it depends on the wholly improbable assumption that the original Welsh narratives were sufficiently current in the eleventh century to be picked up by Breton *conteurs* and carried to France, but that they died out on their home ground and had to be re-introduced in their new French livery sometime in the twelfth century. Few Welsh scholars would now subscribe to this view and there appears to be a broad measure of support for the general drift of Dr Jones's suggestion that the three tales evolved in a bilingual environment in Wales — most likely in the south-east, in Glamorgan and the border areas — during the period after the Norman conquest and that the French influences that are evident in the Welsh texts were absorbed from the actual physical and cultural context in which they were created within Wales itself.[47] This would explain why the Welsh texts are seemingly closer to the common source than Chrétien's, while at the same time Chrétien's texts have elements, including personal names, which are not in the Welsh versions but which clearly derive from earlier Welsh tradition.

To win general acceptance, however, this view of things must be presented in a sufficiently flexible form to account fully for the apparent innovations of the Welsh tales. Brynley F. Roberts, for example, tends to view the Welsh romances as retellings of Chrétien's poems adapted to *the written* cyfarwydd *style;*[48] *there must be doubt,* he comments appositely, *whether the author of* Owein *could have conceived a narrative with the sophisticated chivalric themes of the tensions arising from the topos of courtly love and the hero's self-knowledge, had he not been aware of the developed forms of French romance.*[49] The answer to this crucial question will, of course, depend precisely on how we envisage the literary and socio-cultural environment in south Wales during the twelfth century and how we assess the cultural awareness of Welsh *littérateurs* like those who wrote the extant versions of the romances.

There is still a good deal of uncertainty as to when the Welsh romances were written, but the most reliable opinions range from 1100 to 1200. Unlike their French counterparts their authorship is unknown: it was formerly commonly supposed, on account of their mutual similarity and their correspondence to Chrétien's trilogy, that they were the work of a single author, but in recent years attention has been drawn to certain disparities in their matter and style and in the orthography in which they are recorded, and this has led to a fairly general rejection of the notion of common authorship: at least it seems clear that *Geraint Son of Erbin* was composed and transmitted separately. None the less, when one reads these tales against the general background of Middle Welsh narrative, it is their mutual similarities that strike one most and set them apart from the other tales of *The Mabinogi*.

How different they are from the Four Branches will, I think, be clear even from a bare outline of the contents of *Owain*:

*At Arthur's court in Caer Llion Cynon tells his companions of an abortive adventure which brought him to a strange region of the emperor's dominions. Passing through a beautiful and unfamiliar* countryside he came upon a great shining castle where he was welcomed with much ceremony and hospitality. When he explained to his host that he was seeking whomsoever might challenge him in feats of arms, he was directed to the next stage of his expedition. There he found a monstrous herdsman — black and with one eye and one leg — who sat on top of a mound and at whose signal all the wild animals did obeisance. From this unprepossessing informant he received instructions on how to reach the wondrous well, or fountain, guarded by the Black Knight. By the well he found a great tree, a slab of marble and a silver bowl fastened to a silver chain. Still following the herdsman's instructions he poured a bowl of water on the slab, whereupon there was a resounding peal of thunder followed by a fearsome shower of hail that stripped the tree of its foliage and decimated men and animals. When the sky cleared a flight of birds descended on the tree and sang with unearthly beauty. Just then the guarding knight came to give challenge to Cynon, subjected him to a humiliating defeat and sent him off minus his horse and his self-respect.

On hearing Cynon's tale Owain is spurred to attempt the same adventure. He retraces Cynon's journey, encounters the Black Knight, wounds him and pursues him until they come to a fortified city. Here Owain finds himself trapped between the dropped portcullis and the inner gate, but when it seems that he must be captured and slain he is befriended by a girl who contrives his escape (with the aid of a ring of invisibility). The Black Knight soon dies and Owain falls in love with his widow. Luned, her companion maidservant and Owain's ministering angel, is instrumental in bringing about their meeting and their marriage.

The second half of the tale also commences from Arthur's court. The emperor and his retinue set out in search of Owain and traverse the same ground as Owain and Cynon until they encounter the Black Knight. All the company are defeated by him in single combat until he joins battle with Gwalchmai and is recognized by him as his friend Owain. After the subsequent feasting Arthur obtains the countess's permission to bring Owain back with him to his court for three months, but once there Owain forgets his ties and remains three years. Then a maiden comes to the court and rebukes and disowns him before riding off. Owain *goes off into the wilderness and roams in solitude among the wild animals until finally, when weakened and near to death, he is rescued by another countess and her handmaidens and nursed back to health. He repays her by defending her against the persecution of a neighbouring earl before continuing his own personal pilgrim's progress. He succours a lion, which henceforth becomes his constant companion and protector. He comes upon Luned, who is about to be killed for defending his good name in the countess's household, and as soon as he has slain — as it were in parenthesis — a monstrous being and saved the two sons of a hospitable earl he returns to kill Luned's would-be executioners. Here the tale comes to its natural end with Owain and Luned's return and his reconciliation with the countess, but to it has been appended a new episode telling how Owain overcomes the Black Oppressor (Y Du Traws) and rescues the four-and-twenty fair ladies who were his prisoners.*

There is a great deal in this narrative, particularly in the detail with which it is fleshed out, that has to do with the practices and protocol of knight errantry, and one is conscious of a general veneer of courtly mannerism more formalized than anything we find in the rest of *The Mabinogi*. But perhaps the most striking discrepancy between the romances and the other tales is in their setting. To begin with, Arthur's court is here at Caer Llion rather than at Celli Wig in Cornwall as in *Culhwch and Olwen* and the Welsh triads, a change which may be due to the influence of Geoffrey of Monmouth. But what is still more remarkable is that, instead of the well-defined landscape of the Four Branches with their generous scattering of familiar place-names, here we find ourselves in a land suspended somewhere between dream and reality, a rich and varied terrain in which the hero may happen suddenly on a splendid castle or a populous fortified town and yet which appears as if it were to him a strange and virgin territory once he leaves the precincts of Arthur's court. Owain travels *the bounds of the world and its wilderness* before reaching the castle, the fountain and the fortified town of the countess and the Black Knight, but afterwards he wonders that all this should exist *in the dominions of the Emperor Arthur without its being discovered* — in other words for Owain Arthur's dominions were coterminous with the reaches of the medieval world, known and unknown.

In its paucity of known place-names it recalls the world of the folktale, in its ambivalent amalgam of the actual and the supernatural it is at one with the world of the romantic Celtic hero-tale which bulks so large in Irish literature, particularly in the cycle of Fionn mac Cumhaill and the *fiana. The faculty of abstracting from the land their eyes beheld another Ireland through which they wandered in dream, has always been a characteristic of the Celtic poets* — well might AE (George Russell) use the word 'Celtic', for here indeed we are dealing with a quality that is pan-Celtic rather than merely Irish. The preternatural dimension which perhaps more than anything else gives the Welsh romances their peculiar depth and resonance is rooted deep in insular Celtic tradition, and for the reader familiar with Irish literature its presence throughout the romances requires less explanation than its relative absence in the Four Branches.

This is a matter of some importance in considering the provenance of the Welsh romances, if only because it figures frequently in earlier discussions of their relationship to Chrétien's compositions on the one hand and to the Four Branches on the other. Brynley F. Roberts has given a convenient thumb-nail résumé of the features which have been repeatedly noted as

99

distinguishing the Welsh versions of the romances from the so-called 'native' tales:

*Their special characteristics are usually identified as, for example: Arthur, le roi fainéant; the courtesy and social customs of the court; the logical structure of the 'romances' and their imprecise topography; but more important, though less specific, are the unreal fairy-like quality of the setting, the literary function of the court as an opening scene for adventures, the theme of knight errantry (a loosely linked series of adventures), and the motive of love service, none of which is characteristic of the 'native' stories*[50]

and, like all the other items in the list, the undoubted vagueness of the topography and the otherworldliness of the environment have been invoked from time to time to dissociate the romances from the more 'native' tales and assimilate them to their French counterparts.[51] Even those who did not wholly accept the secondary role assigned to the Welsh versions were sometimes persuaded that these twin features somehow set them apart from the general run of traditional Welsh narrative. It is, however, dangerous in the case of an early vernacular literature to proceed as if we had the totality of evidence before us; it is particularly perilous in the case of Welsh, where the Middle Welsh texts evidently preserve only a tiny proportion of the earlier oral narrative and need not — almost certainly do not — adequately reflect its conceptual-stylistic thematic range. The fact is that the three extant romances belong to the Arthurian cycle of storytelling (notwithstanding the disparate origins of their three heroes, Owain, Geraint and Peredur) and that the cognate Irish cycle of Fionn, which parallels the whole Arthurian tradition in so many respects, is itself characterized by the two very features which scholars have accepted as evidence for the French

100

origin of the three Welsh tales (cf. pp. 122–4 below). The natural inference is that they had always been part of the oral tales associated with the mythico-historical legend of Arthur. Whether the palpable French influence on the spirit and trappings of the three romances constitutes proof of French provenance must, for the time being at least, remain an open question, but the argument in favour of it must surely forego the seeming support of an ambiance *entre deux mondes*.[52]

Stylistically *Owain* stands somewhere between the Four Branches and the other two romances (though this need have no chronological implications). It has essentially the same strong supple prose as the Four Branches, but it is less frugal and restrained in its use of description, though still more sparing of ornate, adjectival language than either *Geraint* or *Peredur*. Structurally it is simpler than the Four Branches and simpler than *Geraint*, to which it is a thematic pendant. The thematic core of *Owain* is Owain's neglect of his wife for the company of Arthur's court, in *Geraint* it is Geraint's neglect of the responsibilities of his own court for the pleasures of Enid's companionship; and in addition to this inverted parallel at the heart of the two tales there is the associated theme of the heroic quest which in both texts draws upon the same store of conventionalized narrative motif. But *Owain* is less complex in structure than *Geraint*. As in traditional oral storytelling the pattern of the story is a linear one: the narrator tells his tale in the actual historical order of its happening, occasionally switching to cyclic or repetitive narrative where someone other than the hero temporarily assumes the principal role. These instances of repeated narrative are turned to good literary effect — and without duplicating the single thread of the continuing events: when Cynon covers part of the same ground as Owain, he does so outside the main narrative and as a motivation for it, and when Arthur and his men retrace the same route this comes precisely at the point where Owain has married the countess and is, as it were, temporarily *hors de combat*, so that the repetition passage serves principally to bring Owain and Arthur together and not to introduce a separate sequence of events.

*Geraint* is by comparison much longer as well as more complex, the one no doubt the product of the other. It falls into three fairly distinct sections: the sequence culminating in Geraint's marriage to Enid, his return to Cornwall where his preoccupation with Enid disgruntles his nobles, and finally his estrangement from Enid and the series of trials which lead to their reconciliation. In the first section there is conscious alternation of episodes featuring different protagonists:

*First there is an account of Arthur's court and his preparations and departure to hunt the marvellous white stag. The narrative then switches to Gwenhwyfar and Geraint who are both late for the hunt, set out separately and meet on the way. They encounter the Knight of the Kestrel and are insulted by the dwarf who accompanies him. Geraint follows the knight till he comes to a strange town and there he meets Earl Ynywl and his daughter (Enid) and resolves their differences with the 'young earl' after defeating the Knight of the Kestrel in the tournament and sending him grievously wounded to Arthur's court. The scene now reverts to Arthur and the hunt, and we are told of the killing of the white stag, the meeting with Gwenhwyfar and the return to the court. Next comes the arrival of the Knight of the Kestrel at the court to make amends for his insult to Gwenhwyfar; he is received kindly and his wounds cared for.*

102

The kind of scene and character switching which we see here is less suited to oral than to written literature, and while there can be no doubt that the romances were composed in their extant form as written texts, for the most part they would have been disseminated through public rather than private reading. This explains why it was felt necessary to mark three successive transitions in the narrative by brief 'stage directions': 'His story so far', 'Geraint's story so far', and 'Their story so far'; abrupt transitions are less disconcerting to the eye than to the ear. They are not used, however, in the remainder of the tale, which follows fairly consistently the fortunes of Geraint:

*Geraint returns with Enid to the court, where they are ceremoniously married. Later, at the request of his father, he goes to his kingdom in Cornwall, defends its boundaries and makes himself renowned for his feats of chivalry. But he begins more and more to devote himself to the pleasures of the court and the company of his wife until his nobles grow discontented. Enid, hearing of this, fears that she is guilty of distracting him from his knightly responsibilities, but her anxiety is misinterpreted by Geraint (with an obtuseness which contrasts sharply with Enid's sensitivity) as indicating that she wishes to give her love to another man. In a magnificent fit of pique he sets off on a peripatetic journey accompanied by Enid whom he refuses to speak to. He emerges successful from a series of fights against odds and on each occasion Enid warns him despite his refusal to hear her. They meet a boy who gives them the food he is bringing to a band of mowers and secures them a lodging in the nearby town (which is unnamed). The earl of that town befriends them. With Geraint's leave he makes advances to Enid, but she remains faithful to Geraint despite his boorishness. She warns him against the earl's plan to kill him and have her for himself and he thwarts his attackers. Grievously wounded he comes upon Arthur's men and defeats Cei before encountering Gwalchmai who recognizes him and has him cared for by Arthur's physicians. Subsequently he*

103

*kills three giants, but is critically wounded and rescued by the Earl of Limwris. Enid rejects the earl's attentions and is sorely mistreated by him. Geraint, though nearer to death than life, kills the earl and is reconciled to Enid. But the tale does not end until Geraint has achieved one final adventure in which he defeats a strange knight and dispels a mist of enchantment.*

Apart from this last supernumerary episode, which is not very coherent in itself nor clearly relevant to what has gone before, *Geraint* has a clear and progressive narrative line. We have seen how in the first section the author switches protagonists and situations without interrupting or complicating the essential movement of the tale. In the third section he introduces a different kind of variation when he describes Geraint and Enid's meeting with the boy who offers them food: this pastoral, almost Hardy-esque, interlude provides a happy relief from the conventional style of the main narrative:

*And after some time they left the forest and came to flat open country, and there were meadows on one side and men with scythes mowing the hay. They came to a river and the horses bent down and drank from it, and from the river they climbed a lofty hill, and there they met a slender young lad with a towel about his neck, and they could see a bundle in the towel but did not know what it was. And he had a small blue pitcher in his hand and a cup over its mouth. And the youth greeted Geraint. 'God prosper you,' said Geraint, 'where do you come from?' 'I come from the town that is there before you. Lord,' said he, 'would you take it ill if I asked you where you come from?' 'I would not,' he replied, 'I came through the forest there.' 'You did not come through it today?' 'No, I spent last night in the forest.' 'I should imagine that you had little comfort there and that you were without food or drink.' 'God knows I had not.' 'Take my advice then and let me give you your meal?' 'What kind of meal?' said Geraint. 'A breakfast I was taking to the mowers over there, nothing other than bread and meat and wine. And if you wish it, sir, they shall go without.' 'I do,' said Geraint, 'and God repay you.'*

*Geraint dismounted, and the youth lifted the girl to the ground. They washed and had their meal, and the youth sliced the bread and gave them drink and served them in everything. And when they had finished he arose and said to Geraint, 'Lord, with your leave I shall go to fetch food for the mowers.'. . .*

This is one of the few incidents in the whole of the three romances for which one cannot readily recall frequent analogues in earlier Celtic literature, and the presumption is that our author is here inventing rather than adapting and that he is consciously seeking to introduce a note of homeliness and naturalness into a heavily stylized context. The effect is to vary the tempo and the temper of the narrative without impairing its continuity.

In this *Geraint*, together with *Owain*, is in marked contrast to the looser and less articulated structure of *Peredur*. Indeed the main preoccupation of the many modern commentators of *Peredur* has been precisely the problem of its structure and whether it should be regarded as a conflation or a unitary text. In the most comprehensive treatment of the tale to appear so far Glenys Goetinck comes to the conclusion that

*provided allowance is made for the effects of time and the efforts of later redactors inspired by the continental romances, it is not difficult to see* Peredur *as one unified piece of work, rather than the uneasy amalgamation of parts proposed by its critics*[53] —

—but still her fairly flexible proviso is a clear ack- nowledgement of the discontinuity of the extant narrative. Even at a casual reading one can, in common with most of the commentators, see that the text comprises three parts. The first of these begins with an account of Peredur's youth and his arrival at Arthur's court to become a knight: the description of his entrance to the court, awkward and unkempt and riding a bony decrepit nag, is a parody of the advent of the future hero, presumptuous and impressive, as it is found in *Culhwch and Olwen* and in Irish tales — it is a good example of the dionysiac urge to turn conventional forms on their heads, which is as old and as deep-seated in Celtic tradition as the conventional forms themselves. Cei, the peevish, opinionated member of Arthur's following, heaps ridicule on the newcomer and maltreats a dwarf and his wife who speak well of him; but when a strange knight does insult to Gwenhwyfar, Arthur's queen, and all the knights of the court hold back in fear, it is this raw and clownish figure who coolly exacts mortal retribution. He takes his departure immediately, promising never to return to Arthur's court until he has avenged Cei's insult to the dwarfs. In the course of his subsequent adventures he comes to several marvellous castles, in one of which, the Castle of Wonders, he sees a spear dripping blood and a severed head on a salver. He encounters two uncles, brothers of his mother, and from them learns courtesy and swordsmanship, and he overcomes the nine witches of Caer Loyw, receives arms from them and is taught by them to ride his horse and to handle his weapons. It is, then, as a fully fledged hero that he meets with Arthur's men, manhandles Cei, and returns to the court.

The second part (which is not represented in the *Perceval* of Chrétien de Troyes) begins when Peredur meets with Angharad Goldenhand at Arthur's court: when she rejects his professions of affection out of hand, he vows never to speak to another Christian until she confesses to loving him more than any other man, and this provides the point of departure for a brief adventure sequence before Peredur returns to court. Cei, not recognizing him immediately, demands to know his identity, and when Peredur's vow prevents him answering, attacks and wounds him without reply or retaliation, and it is only when Angharad declares her love for him that Peredur reveals who he is.

At this point there is a caesura in the narrative after which Peredur goes out to hunt, wanders far afield, comes upon a strange castle, thus signalling a fresh series of adventures and echoing what must have been one of the most familiar motifs in insular Celtic tradition: the hunt which leads the hero to a strange dwelling which is in effect the Otherworld and in which he undergoes extraordinary and often frightening experiences. Most of the many Irish analogues occur in the semi-popular tales of Fionn mac Cumhaill and his *fiana*, and, as we have already noted, the Fionn tradition as a whole shows numerous fundamental parallels to the Arthurian tradition of Britain and may reasonably be regarded as its Irish counterpart: one might therefore infer that versions of these adventures may have been told of Peredur in popular storytelling just as similar tales were told in Ireland — and still are told — of Fionn and Oisín and Caoilte, and that they were gathered in by an author who set the comprehensiveness of his narrative before its unity. Moreover it is also to be noted that Peredur's adventures are made to lead up to the final episode of the section, that in which he forms an alliance with the Empress of Constantinople and rules together with her for fourteen years; for it has been recognized that the Empress is but another of the many literary realizations of the goddess of sovereignty, reflecting one of the most perennial and most dominant concepts of Celtic socio-religious consciousness and one which was commonly associated in insular Celtic tradition with the theme of the hunt which strays from the natural world to the supernatural and which brings hero and goddess together in a sacred union that creates and symbolizes the peace and prosperity of the kingdom.

The third part of *Peredur* poses many problems of reference and interpretation. It opens with the arrival at Arthur's court of a black-visaged woman whose comprehensive ugliness is described in impressive detail. She upbraids Peredur for not enquiring about the meaning of the bleeding spear and the other wonders he had seen at the court of the lame king: had he done so the king would have been restored to health and the land to peace and prosperity. She tells also of a maiden besieged in her castle, declaring that he who would rescue her would win *the highest renown in the world*. Gwalchmai sets out on this venture, but the text follows his fortunes only for a short time before reverting to Peredur, who, for his part, has taken up the dark woman's challenge and resolved to find out the meaning of the bleeding spear. His subsequent adventures bring him finally to the Castle of Wonders where he is informed — with rather more brevity than clarity — about the meaning of the wonders he had witnessed, and the tale ends with Peredur, backed up by Arthur and his war-band, slaying the witches of Caer Loyw. This whole section lacks both consistency and continuity. The connection with the first section is poorly articulated, the roles of Angharad and the Empress ambiguous and uncoordinated, that of Gwalchmai truncated and irrelevant and the several adventures blurred and disjointed; whatever the reason, the author would here seem to have been defeated by the complexity of his sources, and when he dispatches briefly and baldly what ought to have been Peredur's crowning achievement, the encounter with the witches, it is almost as if he were throwing in his hand.

However, despite its being structurally less organized, *Peredur* has the same principal thematic features as the other two romances. The first is the proving of the hero, and in this instance *Peredur* begins at the beginning of the traditional scenario with an account of his birth, youth and initiation before Peredur the ordained knight goes forth like Owain and Geraint to test his prowess against formidable opponents. The whole sequence has many precedents in early Irish literature, and no doubt there were many in early Welsh, but the first two segments of the heroic career — the making and the proving of the hero — are not always combined in a single narrative; there were therefore models in insular tradition for both the variants found in *Peredur* and in the other two romances. In both cases the pattern is old, but upon it there has been superimposed a veneer of usage and expression deriving from the world of courtesy and knight errantry and embracing dress, weapons, armour, fighting, and above all the relations between men and women. And with this last point we come to the second of the two primary features of the romances: the union of the hero and his lady. Here again the roots go deep in the mythic histories of the ancient Celts. Stories clustered around every stage of the hero's career: his birth, his upbringing, his martial training, his feats and adventures, and — not least — his loves and his marriage: and as one who was not divine yet something more than human the hero's liaisons were often with women who were drawn to him from the land of the supernatural. There were difficulties to be overcome, sometimes fearful ordeals and journeys into the realm of the unknown, before the union could be consummated, and already in some of the earliest Irish tales the hero is presented with an agonizing conflict of loyalties, as when Noíse had to choose between Deirdre and his duty to his king, Conlae between the Otherworld woman and his attachment to his father and his people, and Diarmaid ua Duibhne between Gráinne and the leader of his war-band Fionn mac Cumhaill. Herein surely lie the seeds of that tension of love and loyalty which underlies much of Arthurian romance and which is central to our three Welsh tales, even if it is somewhat obscured by the structural disarray of *Peredur*. Here the old conflict has been realized as one between the hero's love for his lady on the one hand and his duty to the knightly ideal and to the court of King Arthur on the other. The externals of the ancient drama may have changed but not its substance.

But there is another aspect of this union of woman and hero which has still greater significance for the social ideology of the Celts. It has been amply demonstrated that the extant romances comprise the remains of ancient dynastic legends, from northern Britain in the case of *Owain* and *Peredur* and from Brittany in the case of *Geraint*, and that they embody one of the most vital concepts of the Celtic peoples: that of the land personified as a woman, a goddess, whose willing union with its ruler confers legitimacy on his rule and peace and fruitfulness upon his kingdom. This myth colours the whole of Irish history, it is deeply imprinted in historical records and literature, and it could be argued that it has affected the very course of historical events. It would be difficult to think of a more dramatic, and dynamic, comment on socio-political change than the recurrent theme of the ugly hag transformed into a beautiful girl through union with her rightful lord; Irish poets and storytellers — including those of Anglo-Ireland — were fascinated by its rich symbolism and for a millennium and a half wrought endless poetic and allegorical variants on it, and if we can bear to look closely at the black and ugly female who comes to rebuke Peredur, we shall easily recognize in her yet another of the countless reflexes of the *puella senilis* whose presence so dominates the Celtic conception of kingship and society.

That the sovereignty myth underlies the three romances is beyond question, but it may be asked whether those who composed the extant texts were fully aware of its deeper significance. In general, the indications are that by the eleventh or twelfth century in Wales the knowledge and understanding of native mythology, even among the learned poets, was patchy and unsystematic, but nevertheless, as in a much later period in Ireland, certain basic concepts seem to have survived the social system which had generated them, and of these the myth of the goddess of sovereignty and of the sacred marriage, the *hieros gamos*, was one of the most permanent and productive. We have noted the role of Eleanor of Aquitaine as promoter and patron of *courtoisie*. When about 1170 Eleanor had her son Richard installed as Duke of Aquitaine, she arranged that this should take the form of a symbolic marriage between him and St Valéry, the legendary martyr and patroness of the region. The saint's ring was placed on his finger *in solemn token of his indissoluble union with the provinces and vassals of*

111

*Aquitaine.* One does not need to be a Celticist to appreciate the implications of this ritual; as one medieval historian comments:

*In this action were combined the attributes of sacred kingship, sacramental initiation and the mysteries of archaic religion. We cannot hope to understand the atmosphere surrounding the courtly romances unless we accept as a fact this close union of the primeval and magical with hard-headed practical politics.*

On this evidence Eleanor would have been quick to see the implications of the sovereignty theme that is woven into the matter of the romances, as no doubt were their authors and the more informed among the audiences who heard them read.

I have remarked elsewhere that, whatever the social position of women in Celtic society, the heroines of Celtic literature are often represented as dominant and even domineering characters and I have suggested that their literary ascendancy is the product of their divinity; for the Celtic heroine is always either divine or shaped after the model of divine archetypes. The result is that, just as the heroic legend of the hero was easily assimilated to the code of chivalry, so was the pre-eminent status accorded to the heroines of Celtic traditions admirably suited to the cult of idealized woman which spread from the south of France — largely through the mediation of Eleanor of Aquitaine — to become an integral part of the world of courtly romance and knighthood. In both cases woman wields an authority that is the antithesis of her normal role in society. She may be aloof, imperious and sometimes wilful, like Owain's countess or Peredur's empress — far less frequently does one find insular correlatives for the docile Enid, though there are some, since the goddess may be gentle and complaisant in one of her several aspects. When she is united with the hero he becomes her consort and her protector, like a well-loved mercenary; he is dedicated to her as he is to Arthur and the heroic brotherhood, and from this polarity spring the tensions that afflict him and which can only be resolved through trials and adventures.

In a sense it is the lady's position rather than her person that makes her sought after by the hero. When Owain saw the countess at a distance *he was fired with love of her that filled every part of him*, but this instant response to his view of her receives little enough support and explanation from the subsequent account of the lady and of his relations with her. The reality is that she was the sovereign ruler and as such it was destined that she should be loved by the appropriate hero. Denis de Rougemont has written of the most famous of all the lovers of medieval romance:

*Tristan and Iseult do not love one another. They say they don't, and everything goes to prove it.* What they love is love and being in love. *They behave as if aware that whatever obstructs love must ensure and consolidate it in the heart of each and intensify it infinitely in the moment they reach the absolute obstacle, which is death. Tristan loves the awareness that he is loving far more than he loves Iseult the Fair. And Iseult does nothing to hold Tristan. All she needs is her passionate dream. Their need of one another is in order to be aflame, and they do not need one another as they are . . .*

and given the differences between *Tristan and Iseult* and the three romances, one can see that his argument has some relevance for them also. Owain and the countess love one another because it is their function to do so, and accordingly it is unnecessary for the

113

author to demonstrate to his readers precisely what makes the lady so irresistibly attractive to Owain. The author himself underlines this point by the care with which he has created the personality of Luned, the countess's companion and servant and surely one of the most sympathetic and best-drawn characters in Welsh literature. She is practical and resourceful: she sees to all Owain's needs promptly and efficiently even before he is aware of them and stage-manages his meeting with the countess. She is witty and well-spoken; for instance when Owain declares his love for her lady, her immediate response is: *'God knows, she loves you not, neither a little or at all.'* She is wholly without affectation, but not without a touch of temper: note how she flares up and speaks her mind when her mistress will not return her greeting.

Indeed this whole passage is a splendid piece of acute observation and lively dialogue: a verbal duel between two quick-witted, articulate women, one of them taking full advantage of her greater authority and social rank, the other compensating by her sheer intelligence and independence of mind. When the countess protests her own great loss and reminds Luned of all the kindnesses she has done her, Luned ignores the reproach and suggests that she would be better advised to seek another husband than to parade her grief for the one she has lost. Despite her lady's feigned anger she knows how to awaken her curiosity, and this gives rise to one of the shrewdest touches in the tale: after some sharp exchanges between the two of them Luned declares that their relationship is irrevocably at an end and makes to leave. But clearly she knows all too well that they are both engaged in a battle of wits and of will, and she counts on the countess rising to her bait — which she does:

*And with that Luned went out, and the countess arose and went to the chamber door after her and coughed aloud, and Luned looked back. The countess gave her a nod and Luned came back to her.*

Owain comes to the arranged meeting with the countess, ostensibly having just arrived from Arthur's court, but the lady — another neat touch this — discerns immediately that he has not the look of a traveller and that he is in fact her husband's killer. But Luned is not at all discountenanced by her discovery, nor indeed is the countess as appalled by it as her expressions of grief would have led one to expect. In fact we are aware throughout that the countess's attitude is compounded of, on the one hand, a righteous grief for her dead husband and anger that anyone should underestimate it, and, on the other, a certain curiosity and expectancy about Luned's plans for her (and even a hidden complicity in them). This is all subtly conveyed without ever being explicitly expressed. These two women know each other's strenghts and weaknesses — and know that they know.

By comparison with these subtle personalities Owain is an honest, sound and rather staid fellow (in this he is typical enough of the hero, who, for all his assurance and daring in the face of physical dangers, tends to become rather insensitive and dull-witted when he intrudes into the domain of women, and particularly as regards all that has to do with marriage and the relations of the sexes). It is remarkable — and no doubt quite deliberate on the part of the author — that Owain does not, so far as the text goes, utter a word at his meeting with the countess: the whole dialogue is monopolized by the two women and one must imagine Owain as a mere pawn looking on passively as his future is decided between these fair and formidable adversaries. His male obtuseness is exposed most blatantly in his relationship with Luned. It is she who rescues him from certain death, and afterwards she shelters and cossets him, prosecutes his suit with the countess, and risks her life to defend his good name against his enemies, while he throughout seems to take her for granted, and this despite the fact that there are clear indications in her words and actions that she is deeply in love with him.

Owain's soberness is pointed up also by the contrast with Cynon, who as we saw anticipates part of Owain's first journey. When Cynon recounts his adventures, he does so with a certain innocent naturalness, which is brought out for example in the way he confirms some of his more striking statements by addressing Cei directly by name: '*And I tell you this, Cei, that is my mind* . . .' and so on. He is full of boyish *naïveté* and frankness: '*I was the only son of my mother and father, and I was high-spirited and full of presumption, and I did not believe that there was anyone in the world who could get the better of me at any kind of feat* . . .' He is impulsive and even tactless: after his welcome in the first castle he arrives at, the host maintains silence until the meal is half over and then enquires after the purpose of his journey; at which, says Cynon, '*I answered that it was high time I had some one who would converse with me, and that there was not a fault in the court so great as their being so poor at conversation.*' He is eager and impatient to test his mettle against all comers, and his impatience is transmitted into the rhythm of the Welsh prose.[54] And in the end when he is defeated and humiliated by the Black Knight, he makes no effort to conceal his sense of complete and utter shame: '*And I confess to you, Cei, it is a wonder I did not melt into a liquid pool for shame at the mockery I got from the black man.'* The character of Cynon, thus created easily and naturally, without any trace of the self-conscious analysis one finds in the French romances, is surely one of the most effective things of its kind in the whole of *The Mabinogi.*

By comparison with *Owain* the story of *Geraint* is told in a consistently more serious vein. It is arguably the best constructed of the three romances, but it lacks the element of self-mockery and the interplay of personalities that for one reader at least makes Owain the most satisfying of the three. In *Peredur* the hero is cast in essentially the same mould as Cynon: rash and impetuous and with a touch of heroic extravagance that reminds one of *Culhwch and Olwen* or some of the early Irish tales — as for example when the empress sends a hundred knights to fetch him and he ties them *as one ties a roebuck* and throws them into the milldyke. There is extravagance also — even in the context of *courtoisie* — in his attitude to women. When Arthur and his men were searching for Peredur, they saw him at a distance and, not recognizing him, sent one after another of their number to enquire who he was: but, *so fixed were Peredur's thoughts on the woman he loved best, he gave him no answer,* and when attacked simply threw him to the ground. He dealt in this way with four-and-twenty knights and even more harshly with Cei, and still *Peredur did not stir from his meditation more than before, despite seeing the press around Cei.* Again, when he goes to take part in a tournament, he sees a beautiful woman looking through the window of a pavilion:

*And he looked hard at the maiden, and great love of her entered into him. And he was thus gazing at her from morning till mid day, and from mid day till evening, and the tournament had then come to an end.*

The same thing happens on the second day and on the third, until his friend the miller strikes him a mighty blow with an axe-handle to wake him from his reverie. Outwardly all this has a superficial resemblance to the cult of woman practised by the trouvères and troubadours, but in the hands of the author of *Peredur* the exotic theme has been wholly assimilated to the more homely genre of humorous burlesque.

Clearly there are differences between the three romances — differences of style and structure and temper — which make it easy to accept that they are not all three the work of a single hand; but as we have seen, they have also many shared features which set them apart from the rest of Middle Welsh prose. Characters, and even narrative situations, occur in two, or in all three, texts. A good example is the character and the role assigned to Cei, that of a blustering meddler who promises more than he can perform and yet who, for some reason, retains the grudging respect of Arthur and his men: one situation which occurs in all three tales is that in which Cei is made to join battle with the hero and is humiliatingly defeated by him, at which point Gwalchmai, always the copybook knight, intervenes, recognizes the hero and accompanies him back to court. Again, in all three tales Arthur is the *roi fainéant* of the French romances who presides over his court and functions as protector and final arbiter of right and wrong, but leaves the deeds of daring to his knights — though the beginnings of this more otiose role may be discerned already in earlier Welsh literature. And if we compare the dramatis personae of the romances with that of the Four Branches we find that they comprise in the one case historical characters of the fifth and sixth centuries and in the other the gods of Celtic Britain and the debris of their mythologies.

And yet, despite the fact that they borrow their characters from history rather than from mythology, the remarkable thing is that the romances are much more suffused with the sense of the supernatural than are the Four Branches. To ask why this should be so is to touch upon a basic duality within the whole Celtic narrative tradition. In Irish this appears most clearly in the discrepancy between the great cycle of tales associated with the Ulstermen and that of Fionn mac Cumhaill and the *fiana*. While both are heroic in the general sense that they are concerned with the deeds of heroes, the Ulster tales are also heroic in the stricter sense that they represent a period of heroic action within an established society and a clearly defined terrain. However fabulous the exploits of the protagonists, the physical setting is real and accessible and the political context a reflection, however distorted, of an actual historical situation. But the motivation of the *fiana* is very different: where the Ulster hero upholds the integrity of the tribal community and its territory, the *féinid* by his membership of the chosen band of warriors and hunters known as *fiana* removes himself from the settled security of the tribal kingdom and gives himself up to the hazardous freedom of that roving brotherhood whose realm begins where social organization ends and where culture gives way to nature. As Marie-Louise Sjoestedt puts it:

*The* féinid *lives on the margin of society, in forest and wilderness*

119

*where the tribal hero adventures only on brief expeditions, the domain of the* Tuatha, *of the people of the* Síde, *the Celtic spirits of the wilderness. He is in constant contact with those mysterious powers which the man who dwells within the tribe, upon the tribal land and close to the hearth, encounters only rarely, in the chaos of* Samain-*eve [Hallowe'en] or by favour of an initiation from the Otherworld. Thus the myths of the* fiana *take us directly into the region of the supernatural. Living on the margin of human affairs, as advanced outposts of the natural world in the supernatural world, the heroes of the* fiana *have a part in both these worlds and a double character.*[55]

Whereas in the Ulster tales the relations between the two worlds tend to be concentrated at certain specific points of time — the great calendar festivals, for instance, or occasions of initiation ritual — in the case of the *fiana* they are casual and continual. Their predilection for the hunt brings them not only to the furthest outlands of Ireland but also beyond the confines of the natural into the supernatural world. When they set out for the chase, this is but the prelude to some marvellous encounter with Otherworld beings: time after time they come upon ordinary-looking habitations which house a world of wonder and magic and in which they undergo stern trials of their resolution and valour, just as the Arthurian champions happen upon strange courts where they are wondrously feasted and subjected to tests of their wisdom and fortitude. The ambivalent and un-organized character of this order of existence has much in common with the rich and vital resources of popular religion and superstition that underlie the crust of official doctrine and ritual — even in our own century this merging of the two worlds has been noted as a feature of life in old-style rural Ireland — and it is not without significance that the cycle of Fionn mac

120

Cumhaill, like the tales told of Arthur in Wales before the time of Geoffrey of Monmouth, seems to have enjoyed its greatest currency and popularity in the sub-literary world of oral tradition. While among the men of learning in both countries the mythology itself was becoming fragmented and fossilized with the consolidation of Christianity, the mythological ethos retained its vitality unimpaired in the custom and beliefs of the population at large. And one of the features of popular Christian and para-Christian religion in Ireland is — as undoubtedly it once was in Wales — that it tends to be dominated by the goddesses who were rooted in the soil and in the local landscape and who controlled the fertility of the land, as also its sovereignty, and it is perhaps not unreasonable to suppose that this also had something to do with the markedly feminine quality that distinguished commentators have discerned in the three romances.

Notwithstanding the probable historicity of Arthur himself, the complex of legend that eventually became associated with his name corresponds in many essentials to the Irish cycle of the once divine Fionn. In comparison with the uncompromisingly heroic temper of the Ulster tales the stories of Fionn and his *fiana* and of Arthur and his knights are shot through with a romanticism which is no doubt conditioned by the environment in which they took shape and the channels through which they were transmitted. They also have a marked lyric strain which they share in Celtic tradition with anchorites and madmen and other groups and individuals who have their essential being outside the confines of ordered society in a realm where nature has primacy and where sacred and profane are constantly fused. And it is precisely the imaginative freedom that derives from this, the sense of the meeting and blending of the contemporary world with the primeval world when historical limitations of time and space were still without meaning, that gives the Arthurian romances much of their resonance and suggestive power. To the Europe of the twelfth and thirteenth centuries they opened up a whole new universe of the imagination, a forest of symbols waiting to be explored by men of insight and of spiritual as well as physical fortitude, and from the deep well of their traditional sources they assimilated something of the exemplary power of myth: when, for example, Peredur learned the unfortunate consequences of his neglecting to ask the vital questions of his mysterious host, he immediately set forth to brave all the perils of the unknown in order to repair his omission, and in doing so provided a paradigm to be followed by adventurous spirits of all subsequent ages.

Ernest Renan has written of the Celtic preoccupation with the 'adventure', that pursuit of the unknown that had its historical reflex in the endless peregrinations of the Celtic saints and its literary reflex in the numerous accounts of journeys to the Otherworld and in the wide-ranging voyage literature, pagan and Christian, that culminated in the celebrated Voyage of Saint Brendan. This impulse was already old in that 'mythogenetic moment' of British history, the period from *c.* AD 450 to *c.* AD 550 when the Romans had withdrawn and the island was conquered by the Angles, Jutes and Saxons, and it continued unabated in the orally transmitted ideology of the British until in the twelfth century it received a universal dramatic expression in the sudden profuse flowering of Arthurian romance. It is this notion of the quest, following in the footsteps of Peredur, Owain or Geraint through the *sacred forest, pathless and unbounded*, that has inspired countless generations of Europeans and created an unending moment of symbolic renewal in art and literature, like a stone dropped into a quiet pool. The point has been made with convincing sincerity by a modern novelist:

*The extraordinary change in European culture that took place under the influence of the British — in the original Celtic sense of the word — imagination has never, I suspect, been fully traced or acknowledged. The mania for chivalry, courtly love, mystic and crusading Christianity, the Camelot syndrome, all these we are aware of — a good deal too aware, perhaps, in the case of some recent travesties of that last centre of the lore. But I believe that we also owe — emotionally and imaginatively, at least — the very essence of what we have meant ever since by the fictional, the novel and its children, to this strange northern invasion of the early medieval mind. One may smile condescendingly at the naïveties and primitive technique of stories such as Eliduc; but I do not think any writer of fiction can do so with decency — and for a very simple reason. He is watching his own birth.*[56]

The story of Eliduc to which John Fowles refers is told in one of the *lais* of Marie de France, who was active in the late twelfth century, and it is a fact of history that it was through the continental versions of British traditions that the influence which he affirms was mediated to the European world. It is none the less arguable that the impact of the *matière de Bretagne* owed less to the form imposed on it by its secondary authors on the continent than to the innate dynamic of its content. Certainly, despite the greater sophistication and conscious psychological complexity of the continental versions of the romances, as examples of sheer storytelling skill they hardly bear comparison with their Welsh counterparts. These are alive with colour and movement, constantly varying the pace and style of their narrative and employing all the traditional devices of Celtic storytelling — repetition, rhetorical description, hyperbole, and so on — with a freshness that belies their antiquity. They have wit and a touch of self-mockery that compare favourably with the frequent *longeurs* and pretentious digressions of Chrétien's text. They are unmistakably within the mainstream of native literary tradition, but at the same time they have a certain polish and spaciousness, a refinement and extension of traditional themes which are the fruit of the continental element in their making. No doubt it is for reasons such as these that Saunders Lewis has qualified the trilogy of romances as constituting perhaps the greatest achievement of Welsh prose in the Middle Ages. It is a judgement that the present writer would not care to challenge.

As for *The Mabinogi* as a whole, it is surely a remarkable phenomenon however we view it. I have cautiously suggested that the very practice of writing narrative was an innovation in Welsh, perhaps of the tenth or eleventh century; in any event all the indications are that written narrative was, to say the least, uncommon before that period. And yet here we see, within roughly the span of a century and a half, the emergence of an extraordinary miscellany of sophisticated and imaginative prose that has hardly been equalled in the subsequent history of the language. The explanation is, no doubt, that the art of storytelling is as old as the British language and that what survives in writing is but the tip of a mighty iceberg without which it could never have become visible to the eyes of men. The shifting luxuriant tangle of themes and characters and the stylistic usage that have gone to the making of *The Mabinogi* are the product of an evolution extending back over many centuries, and it is important to remember that the teeming profusion of this oral literature is only very inadequately reflected in the written texts of Middle Welsh: the *matière de Bretagne* that looms behind the continental romances owes little, if anything, to *The Mabinogi* as we know them, but represents rather the whole rich accumulation of insular myth and story which was available to the Welsh storyteller, and indeed to his Cornish and Breton colleagues.

In a sense, therefore, the tales of *The Mabinogi* are

merely a by-product of the historical progression of Welsh literary tradition. The learned poets, who were so influential in moulding received opinion on literary matters, paid scant heed to them and would probably have regarded them as relative trivia which had little enough to do with the essential of serious literary activity, which was for them, naturally, the composition of praise-poems and related verse-forms. If the truth be told, *The Mabinogi* seems to have attracted little notice among Welsh men of learning until such time as it benefited from the general revival of interest in native antiquities that came in the wake of the eighteenth-century romantic movement. There is, indeed, a strange irony in the fact — however readily it may be explained — that Welsh poetry had little or no impact abroad though it reigned supreme at home, while traditional prose narrative, tolerated rather than cherished by the native literati, should have conquered the conquerors and won unending fame and influence among the nations of the continent, so that in the event (to quote the words of Lady Charlotte Guest, first translator of *The Mabinogi*) *the Cymric nation . . . has strong claims to be considered the cradle of European romance.*

# Notes

[1] THE PENGUIN BOOK OF WELSH VERSE (Harmondsworth, 1967), 13.

[2] E.g. C. M. Bowra, HEROIC POETRY (London, 1964), 15 f.

[3] For a statement of the theory and a number of relevant references see Myles Dillon, THE ARCHAISM OF IRISH TRADITION, The Sir John Rhŷs Memorial Lecture, British Academy, 1947, 9–11. For a more detailed assessment of it and of the prosimetrum form in insular Celtic literature cf. P. Mac Cana in EARLY IRISH LITERATURE—MEDIA AND COMMUNICATION/MÜNDLICHKEIT UND SCHRIFTLICHKEIT IN DER FRÜHEN IRISCHEN LITERATUR, ed. Stephen N. Tranter and Hildegard L.C. Tristram (Tübingen, 1989), 125–47.

[4] Sir Ifor Williams, THE POEMS OF LLYWARCH HEN, The Sir John Rhŷs Memorial Lecture, British Academy, 1932, 10–12; LECTURES ON EARLY WELSH POETRY (Dublin, 1944), 18 ff.

[5] Cf. P. Mac Cana, op. cit., 139 ff.

[6] ÉRIU, 24 (1973), 90 ff.

[7] The noun-first order is in fact much commoner in modern spoken Welsh than has generally been supposed, but it belongs there to a marked not a neutral style and is especially characteristic of spoken narrative; cf. P. Mac Cana, 'Further notes on constituent order in Welsh', in STUDIES IN BRYTHONIC WORD ORDER, ed. James Fife and Erich Poppe (Amsterdam/Philadelphia, 1991), 45–80.

[8] Cf. E. G. Bowen, THE SETTLEMENTS OF THE CELTIC SAINTS IN WALES (Cardiff, 1954), 33: *If we adopt the*

*conventional division of Britain into a Highland and a Lowland Zone separated by a line joining the mouth of the Tees to that of the Exe, we appreciate at a glance that the position of south-east Wales is that of a western projection of Lowland Britain into the Highland Zone. This all-important fact of physical geography is clearly reflected in the unmistakable association of this region throughout the ages with the cultural life of Lowland Britain.*

[9] Op. cit., 44; SAINTS, SEAWAYS AND SETTLEMENTS IN THE CELTIC LANDS (Cardiff, 1969), 61.

[10] SAINTS, SEAWAYS AND SETTLEMENTS, 38, 39, 106, 108.

[11] THE CHURCH IN EARLY IRISH SOCIETY (London, 1966), 73 f.

[12] Bobi Jones, Y TAIR RHAMANT (Aberystwyth, 1960), xiv; Glenys Goetinck, PEREDUR: A STUDY OF WELSH TRADITION IN THE GRAIL LEGENDS (Cardiff, 1975), 35; Idris Ll. Foster, ARTHURIAN LITERATURE IN THE MIDDLE AGES, ed. R. S. Loomis (Oxford, 1959), 205.

[13] Constance Bullock-Davies, PROFESSIONAL INTERPRETERS AND THE MATTER OF BRITAIN (Cardiff, 1966), 14 f. For the suggested identification of the two Maries see also John Charles Fox, THE ENGLISH HISTORICAL REVIEW, 25 (1910), 303–6, 26 (1911), 317–26; Constance Bullock-Davies, 80 (1965), 314–22, and references in 314 n. 2. The identification is rejected by Philippe Ménard, LES LAIS DE MARIE DE FRANCE (Paris, 1979), 15–17.

[14] Op. cit., 18.

[15] G. J. Williams, TRADDODIAD LLENYDDOL MORGANNWG (Cardiff, 1948), 176.

[16] LLÊN CYMRU 9, 230–3; YSGRIFAU BEIRNIADOL 5, ed. J. E. Caerwyn Williams (1970), 30–43; Y TRAETHODYDD, July 1969, 137–42, October 1969, 185–92. All four essays have since been reprinted in R. Geraint Gruffydd (ed.), MEISTRI'R CANRIFOEDD: YSGRIFAU . . . GAN SAUNDERS LEWIS (Cardiff, 1973), 1–33.

[17] TRANS. HON. SOC. CYMM., 1970, 263 ff.

[18] Rachel Bromwich has suggested that *mabinogi* 'a tale of youth' came to mean *a tale of descendants* and that the Four Branches are *fundamentally the stories of the old Brittonic gods from whom the Welsh dynasties in early historical times claimed descent* (STUDIES IN EARLY BRITISH HISTORY (Cambridge, 1959), 103; TRIOEDD YNYS PRYDEIN: THE WELSH TRIADS (Cardiff, 1961), lxxxvii). Certainly her succinct definition of the four tales is a useful one.

[19] TRANS. HON. SOC. CYMM., 1975, 243 ff.

[20] Pryderi might even be regarded as a variant epiphany of the god Mabon. But, in any case, the transfer of themes and story-patterns from one hero to another is commonplace in Celtic literature.

[21] 'The structure of the Four Branches of the Mabinogi', TRANS. HON. SOC. CYMM., 1975, 250 ff.

[22] THE INTERNATIONAL POPULAR TALE AND EARLY WELSH TRADITION (Cardiff, 1961), 86 ff.

[23] Wendy Doniger O'Flaherty, WOMEN, ANDROGYNES, AND OTHER MYTHICAL BEASTS (Chicago, 1980), 5, 10.

[24] The last ten or fifteen years have been prolific of discretely focused studies contributing to our better understanding of *The Mabinogi*. Several are mentioned in relation to specific points raised in the course of the present essay. As for the rest, some would figure prominently in any extended and detailed assessment of the Four Branches, and all of them, taken together, testify to the wide variety of viewpoints from which the text has already been scrutinized. For example, Katherine McKenna presents *Pwyll* as a tale constructed around the myth of sovereignty but with an exemplary message for Welsh rulers of the period when it was probably composed, *c.* 1060–1120 (THE BULLETIN OF THE BOARD OF CELTIC STUDIES, 29 (1982), 35–52); Patrick Ford illustrates how a shift in one's

immediate perspective may affect one's perception and presentation of the work: dealing with the Four Branches as a whole, he concludes that each *represents a collection of more or less related lore*, which explains *why the quality of the redactor's work is so high within individual sections and episodes, and why continuity between these sections is often lacking or poor* (THE MABINOGI AND OTHER MEDIEVAL WELSH TALES (Berkeley, Los Angeles, 1977), 4), while, turning to *Branwen* in particular, he adopts a rather more integrationist approach and discerns in the text a considerable degree of thematic and conceptual unity (STUDIA CELTICA, 22/23 (1987–8), 29–41); Roberta L. Valente glosses the actions and interaction of Gwydion and Aranrhod in *Math* in terms of their transgression of the gender rules assigned them by social convention (BBCS, 35 (1988), 1–9); John Carey, re-assessing *Math*, believes *that the tale's primary significance is inherited, not synchronic,* as held by several recent commentators, and that it continues, in somewhat altered form, a myth of origins *describing the end of a paradisal state of being, and the emergence of the conditions of morality* (HISTORY OF RELIGIONS, 31 (1991), 24–38; John T. Koch presents some etymologies of proper names with a bearing on the mythology of *The Four Branches* (PROCEEDINGS OF THE HARVARD CELTIC COLLOQUIUM, 9 (1989), 1–11, and in other studies endeavours to demonstrate the underlying equivalence of Manawydan to the early British Mandubracius of Caesar's DE BELLO GALLICO and of the story of Brân/Bendigeidfran's death in *Branwen* to that of the fatal expedition of Brennus to Greece and to Delphi in the winter of 279-8 BC (CMCS, 14 (1987), 17–52, 20 (1990), 1–20); Juliette Wood examines folklore elements in the first branch, concentrating on the motif of the Calumniated

130

Wife and the contemporary relevance of the notion of foreignness (CMCS, 10 (1985), 25–38); Andrew Welsh furnishes a *catalogue raisonné* of traditional motifs, 'international' and 'Celtic', in *The Four Branches* (CMCS, 15 (1988), 51–62), seeks to document the judicious use of popular themes to create a coherent narrative in *Pwyll* by an author well versed in traditional storytelling (CMCS, 17 (1989), 15–41), traces the ramifications, implicit and explicit, of the themes of 'doubling' and incest (Pwyll and Arawn, Gwydion and Gilfaethwy, Gwydion and Aranrhod) and speculates on their psycho-sociological signifiance (SPECULUM, 65 (1990), 344–61), and, finally, construes the story of Branwen in terms of the Germanic 'peaceweaver' represented by two of the female characters in BEOWULF (VIATOR, 22 (1991), 1–13); Sioned Davies tries to apply to the prose of *The Mabinogi* the theories of Milman Parry and Albert B. Lord on the use of formulae in metrical compositions (YSGRIFAU BEIRNIADOL, 14 (Dinbych, 1988), 115–33; PEDEIR KEINC Y MABINOGI (Caernarfon, 1989), 30–45); Glenys Goetinck reflects on the temper and motivations of the characters of the Four Branches and on their implications for the status and purpose of their author (LLÊN CYMRU, 15 (1987–8), 249–69).

One thing this impressive and by no means exhaustive list demonstrates is the great diversity of avenues by which the would-be interpreter may approach *The Four Branches*, thus mirroring something of the multiplicity of the matter and provenance of the compilation; as with other such texts, how one approaches it will generally depend on one's particular expertise, and even one's preferences and preconceptions, rather than on any insistent and unambiguous claim from the text itself. To acknowledge this is not to opt for a position of critical

131

neutrality or indifferentism, but simply to accept that while most approaches have their own degrees of validity, none is complete and definitive, and a satisfactory and comprehensive commentary on *The Four Branches*, when it comes, must of necessity be a flexible synthesis reflecting the heterogeneous character of the text's origins and composition. Andrew Welsh has noted, quite correctly, the 'ambivalence' one finds in the writings of some commentators — including the present one — on *The Four Branches*, but he does acknowledge that this may be in some sense a response suited to the text: *In contrast to much medieval literature, the narrative of* The Four Branches *appears to be itself radically ambivalent about its values, and the characters within the narrative haunted by duality* (SPECULUM, 65 (1990), 344, 347). I would merely venture to suggest that the dualism with which he is concerned in this essay ('doubling and incest') is encompassed within a much larger textual and conceptual complexity.

[25] Cf. Glyn Jones, THE BULLETIN OF THE BOARD OF CELTIC STUDIES, 25 (1974), 380 ff.

[26] The present writer discussed the complexity of the text over thirty years ago in a little book which concerned itself primarily with the question of its possible borrowings from Irish, BRANWEN DAUGHTER OF LLŶR: A STUDY OF THE IRISH AFFINITIES AND OF THE COMPOSITION OF THE SECOND BRANCH OF THE MABINOGI (Cardiff, 1958). As a rounded study of the extant narrative of *Branwen* it was, of course, methodologically quite unsound — as Professor Patrick Ford has recently very correctly observed, its approach is 'misguided from the outset' (STUDIA CELTICA, 22–3 (1987–8), 31). It suffers not only from the fact that it was written by the merest tyro in Welsh studies, but also that it is simply an expansion of a

lecture delivered in response to an invitation that came complete with title: 'The Irish borrowings in *Branwen'*, so that what began as a limited exercise in source-hunting came to masquerade as a full-blown study of the tale. On the other hand, notwithstanding its obvious limitations and defects, there are some fairly central points in its commentary on the structure and development of the extant narrative to which, on more mature and, one hopes, wiser reflection, I would still adhere. One or two of these are represented in the summary account on pp. 25–7.

[27] RHIANNON (Cardiff, 1953), 4.

[28] Op. cit., 6.

[29] Ifor Williams, PEDEIR KEINC Y MABINOGI (Caerdydd, 1930), xxii, xxxiii, xxxix; cf. Glenys Goetinck, LLÊN CYMRU, 15 (1987–8), 253.

[30] Kenneth Hurlstone Jackson, The INTERNATIONAL POPULAR TALE AND EARLY WELSH TRADITION (Cardiff, 1961), 129 f., 86 ff. Dr Seán Ó Coileáin in a recent article complements Jackson's study with a penetrating thematic analysis of *Pwyll* (STUDIA CELTICA, 12–13 (1977–8)). He reveals a remarkable correspondence between the narrative incidents of the two parts of the tale. If I follow his argument correctly, the presumption is that the final outcome of the basic narrative sequence in the first part was aborted by the introduction of the theme of the Chaste Friend/Brother and that this led to the sequence being repeated *ab initio*, but with different surface detail, until its final accomplishment in the birth of Gwri/Pryderi. I have but two observations on this extremely useful study. First, in assessing the significance of thematic correspondences, one must have regard to the element of predictability, especially in medieval and semi-traditional tales in which feasts, feuds, journeys and encounters with enemies are

commonplace; schematic lists of correspondences can look deceptively impressive when divorced from their context. Nevertheless, I find myself almost wholly persuaded by Dr Ó Coileáin's argument here. Secondly, assuming the correctness of his thematic analysis, is the inference he draws the most probable one? One might for instance conclude that there were coexisting birth-tales, those of Pryderi and Gwri, and that the extant tale arose from their fusion. In that case the theme of the Chaste Friend/Brother would have functioned as a linking rather than as a distorting element.

[31] Even such a perceptive scholar as Andrew Welsh is nervous of such a distinction: *There is a curious ambivalence, as some of those interpretations acknowledge, in a critical approach that admires the accomplishment of an author's style even as it argues that his story is badly in need of reconstruction* (SPECULUM, 65 (1990), 344). It is true that we tend to associate the gift of style with that of structure and to expect both of a good poet or author, yet the combination is not universally consistent, whether in modern or medieval literature. All Celticists are familiar with Matthew Arnold's pertinent observation that the remarkable lyric flair of the insular Celts was not matched by a comparable sense of *architectonicé*, and surely it is a disparity of a similar, if not precisely the same order which accounts for the fact that great short-story writers frequently make only moderate novelists. Moreover, in the case of *The Four Branches* I think it is reasonable to assume that its author had more complete control over its style than over the narrative constituents that went to its making.

[32] This and several other of my quotations from *The Four Branches* are taken from THE MABINOGION, translated by Gwyn Jones and Thomas Jones (London,

134

1949).

[33] See, however, Patrick Sims-Williams, 'Riddling Treatment of the "Watchman Device" in *Branwen* and *Togail Bruidne Da Derga'*, STUDIA CELTICA, 12–13 (1977–8), 83 ff., esp. 93–107.

[34] Sir Ifor assumes that she invited the wise men, hoping to learn the truth from them (PEDEIR KEINC Y MABINOGI, ed. Sir Ifor Williams (Cardiff, 1974), 145), but she already knew the truth, or most of it, and in any case the text gives no indication that she made any enquiry of the wise men except with regard to the nature of her penance.

[35] Humour in a foreign environment is notoriously difficult to identify when we lack the reaction of the initiates. One passage that has been cited (by Sir Ifor Williams) as an outstanding example of humour in the Four Branches is that in which Manawydan, returning from Ireland with his fellow-survivors, meets a group of men and women. *'Have you any news?'* said Manawydan. *'No,'* said they, *'except that Caswallawn son of Beli has conquered the Island of the Mighty and is a crowned king in London.'* In other words nothing had happened except the worst possible thing that could have happened: the usurpation of Bendigeidfran's kingdom by Caswallawn.

Is this intended to be humorous? Hardly. It has the disarming negative followed by the devastating positive that characterizes many modern jokes, but I would suspect that in medieval spoken Welsh, as in modern spoken Irish (*Níl, murab é go . . .* 'No, except (perhaps) that . . .'), the pattern of positive response preceded by initial negative was fairly common and therefore lacked the contradictory impact that it has in modern English. More important, however, if this is humour, then it is surely misplaced. The narrative which immediately precedes and

135

follows is wholly serious, not to say tragic, and to read this sentence as humour is to render it wholly incongruous in its context.

To dwell on this single instance may seem like cracking a nut with a sledge-hammer, but the anatomy of the author's humour (or his lack of it) is important for an understanding of his writing, and, in any case, one should always on principle question the passing judgements of outstanding scholars: all too easily do they acquire the status of divine writ. As for Sir Ifor Williams, his own sense of humour was so rich and spontaneous that he could easily exaggerate it in others.

[36] 'La quatrième branche du Mabinogi et la théologie des trois fonctions', in RENCONTRES DES RELIGIONS, ed. Proinsias Mac Cana and Michel Meslin (Paris, 1986), 25–38; also in Georges Dumézil, L'OUBLI DE L'HOMME ET L'HONNEUR DES DIEUX (Paris, 1985), 93–111.

[37] *Ceinciau'r Mabinogi* (Bangor, 1975).

[38] S. Lewis, MEISTRI'R CANRIFOEDD, ed. R. Geraint Gruffydd (Cardiff, 1973), 20.

[39] The complete text of *The Mabinogi* is now preserved only in the Red Book of Hergest. Evidently the White Book of Rhydderch formerly contained the whole text, but in its present state it has only part of *Culhwch and Olwen*, as also of *Lludd and Llefelys* and *Owain*, while *The Dream of Rhonabwy* is completely missing.

[40] For a detailed discussion of the two catalogues in *Culhwch and Olwen* as a reflection of traditional Welsh learning, see Doris Edel, THE BULLETIN OF THE BOARD OF CELTIC STUDIES, 30 (1982–3), 253–67.

[41] Cf. Brynley F. Roberts (ed.), CYFRANC LLUDD A LLEFELYS (Dublin, 1975), xxviiff.

[42] Dr P. P. Sims-Williams has a fine discussion of the enduring medieval notion of the Island of Britain as a pristine unity which was broken as the result of a

series of conquests or oppressions (*gormesoedd*), some of them historical, like the invasion of the Anglo-Saxons, others wholly mythical (in HISTORY AND HEROIC TALE, ed. Tore Nyberg *et al.* (Odense, 1985), 97–131).

[43] George H. Brewer and Bedwyr Lewis Jones, 'Popular tale motifs and historical tradition in *Breudwyt Maxen'*, MEDIUM AEVUM, 44 (1975), 23–30.

[44] TRANS. HON. SOC. CYMM., 1970–1, 266. For an excellent discussion of the satirical intent of the tale as reflected in its structure and style see Dafydd Glyn Jones, in Y TRADDODIAD RHYDDIAITH YN YR OESOEDD CANOL (Llandysul, 1974), 176–95. This has since been supplemented by Edgar M. Slotkin's scrutiny of the text in the light of modern narrative theory, with particular emphasis on the role of the extended descriptions and of the frame within the story (CAMBRIDGE MEDIEVAL CELTIC STUDIES, 18 (1989), 89–111).

[45] THE GAELIC STORY-TELLER, The Sir John Rhŷs Memorial Lecture, British Academy, 1945, 45. For instances of the motif in Scottish Gaelic folklore see Kenneth Jackson, ÉTUDES CELTIQUES, 11 (1964–5), 94 f.

[46] LLÊN CYMRU, 4 (1956–7), 208–27.

[47] Cf. Rachel Bromwich, in Y TRADDODIAD RHYDDIAITH YN YR OESOEDD CANOL, ed. Geraint Bowen (Llandysul, 1974), 158–61, 174; R. L. Thomson, *Owein, or Chwedl Iarlles y Ffynnawn* (Dublin, 1968, 1975), lvii–lxxxiv, esp. lxxxiv; Idris Foster, in Y TRADDODIAD RHYDDIAITH, ed. Geraint Bowen (Llandysul, 1970), 21. For further thoughts by Dr Jones on this subject see now PROCEEDINGS OF THE SEVENTH INTERNATIONAL CONGRESS OF CELTIC STUDIES, OXFORD, 1983, ed. D. Ellis Evans *et al.* (Oxford, 1986), 171–5.

[48] ORAL TRADITION, 3 (1988), 77.

[49] In THE LEGEND OF ARTHUR IN THE MIDDLE AGES, ed.

P. B. Grout *et al.* (Cambridge, 1983), 180; also YSGRIFAU BEIRNIADOL, ed. J. E. Caerwyn Williams, 15 (1988), 29–45.

[50] In THE LEGEND OF ARTHUR etc., ed. P. B. Grout *et al.* (Cambridge, 1983), 179.

[51] Notably J. D. Bruce, THE EVOLUTION OF ARTHURIAN ROMANCE (Göttingen and Baltimore, 1923), i, 47, 70.

[52] One might almost say the same for the notion that the representation of Arthur as a *roi fainéant* links the Welsh romances to Chrétien's poem rather than to native Arthurian storytelling. Not only is the relevant Welsh narrative material too limited in scope to permit such a confident distinction, but it could be fairly argued that the Arthur of *Culhwch and Olwen* already betrays clear signs of the shift from the active warrior leader to the inactive presiding and guiding chief. What is more, the same change of role is well attested for his Irish congener, Fionn mac Cumhaill, and would seem to have its roots in insular literary tradition.

[53] PEREDUR: A STUDY OF WELSH TRADITION IN THE GRAIL LEGENDS (Cardiff, 1975), 21.

[54] Cf. OWEIN, ed. R.L. Thomson (Dublin, 1968), ll. 117ff.

[55] Marie-Louise Sjoestedt, GODS AND HEROES OF THE CELTS, translated from the French by Myles Dillon (London, 1949), 84–5.

[56] John Fowles, THE EBONY TOWER (Panther Books, 1974), 120.

# The Author

Proinsias Mac Cana was born in Belfast in 1926. He was educated at The Queen's University of Belfast and continued his postgraduate studies at the Sorbonne and Dublin. From 1951 to 1955 he was Assistant Lecturer and Lecturer in Queen's University and from 1955 to 1961 Lecturer in Old and Middle Irish in the University College of Wales, Aberystwyth. In 1961 he was appointed a professor in the School of Celtic Studies of the Dublin Institute for Advanced Studies and in 1963 became Professor of Welsh in University College, Dublin. In 1971 he was appointed to the Chair of Early (including Medieval) Irish in the same college. In 1985 he returned as a Senior Professor to the Dublin Institute for Advanced Studies, and from 1987 to 1992 he was also Annual Visiting Professor (first semester) in the Department of Celtic Languages at Harvard University. He was President of the Royal Irish Academy, 1979–82. He has written extensively on Celtic language, literature and religion, and his publications include BRANWEN DAUGHTER OF LLŶR (University of Wales Press, 1958), CELTIC MYTHOLOGY (London, 1970) and THE LEARNED TALES OF MEDIEVAL IRELAND (Dublin, 1980).

Most of the quotations from *The Mabinogi* in this essay are based upon the translation in Everyman's Library by Gwyn Jones and Thomas Jones, *The Mabinogion* (London, New York, 1949, new edition 1974). The author wishes to thank Professor Gwyn Jones and Mrs Mair Jones for permission to use these quotations.

*Designed by Jeff Clements.*
*Typeset by the National Library of Wales, Aberystwyth, in*
*Palatino 11pt on 13pt and printed in Great Britain by*
*Qualitex Printing Limited, Cardiff, 1992.*

---

British Library Cataloguing in Publication Data

A catalogue record for this book is available from the British Library.

ISBN 0-7083-1109-1

First edition 1977
Second edition 1992

Published with the financial support of the Welsh Arts Council